Blick nach Osten.

Versuch der Konstruktion einer chinesischen Hermeneutik

Handing Hong

Blick nach Osten.

Versuch der Konstruktion einer chinesischen Hermeneutik

Herausgegeben von Hongjian Wang

Impressum

Handing Hong

Blick nach Osten.

Versuch der Konstruktion einer chinesischen Hermeneutik

Reihe: Interpretation und Praxis — Bd. 1

Herausgegeben von Hongjian Wang

ISBN 978-3-942106-85-6

© 2023 xenomoi verlag, Berlin

Satz in Palatino Linotype 11 Pt.

Umschlaggestaltung, Satz und Produktion:
xenomoi verlag e.K., Heinersdorfer Str. 16, D - 12209 Berlin
Tel.: 030 - 755 11 712 • www.xenomoi.de • info@xenomoi.de

Bibliographische Information der Deutschen Nationalbibliothek:
Die Deutsche Nationalbibliothek verzeichnet diese Publikation in der
Deutschen Nationalbibliographie; detaillierte bibliografische Daten
sind abrufbar im Internet über
http://dnb.d-nb.de.

This book is supported by the Research Center for Chinese and Western Classical Hermeneutics, Hunan University.

Über den Autor und den Herausgeber:

Handing Hong, geboren 1938, ist Ehrendoktor der Universität Düsseldorf und der chinesische Übersetzer von *Wahrheit und Methode*. Zu seinen deutschsprachigen Abhandlungen gehören *Spinoza und die deutsche Philosophie. Untersuchung zur metaphysischen Wirkungsgeschichte des Spinozismus in Deutschland* (1989) und *Chinesische Philosophie. Eine Einführung* (2008, mit Lutz Geldsetzer).

Hongjian Wang, geboren 1989, ist Doktor der Philosophie an der Universität Freiburg. Er ist der Autor von *Ontologie der Praxis bei Martin Heidegger* (2020) und *Martin Heidegger. Perspectives on the Interpretation of his Thinking* (2021).

Inhaltsverzeichnis

Der Besuch von Handing Hong bei Gadamer und die Frage nach der chinesischen Hermeneutik

Der Besuch von Prof. Handing Hong bei Herrn Prof. Gadamer im Jahr 2001 kann als ein wichtiges Ereignis in der Geschichte des chinesisch-westlichen hermeneutischen Austauschs angesehen werden. Kurz nach diesem Interview verfassten Herr Hong und Herr Lutz Geldsetzer, ein anderer Teilnehmer dieses Besuchs, separate Berichte über das Ereignis, die in den wichtigsten Medien in China und in Deutschland veröffentlicht wurden. Professor Geldsetzer zeichnete den Besuch auf Video auf und der Inhalt dieses Videos wurde 2021 von Dr. Karl Kraatz transkribiert.

Ich war einer der Ersten, die das betreffende Manuskript zu Gesicht bekamen. Um ehrlich zu sein, war ich zunächst einmal enttäuscht von dem, was in diesem Text präsentiert wurde. Für diese Enttäuschung gibt es verschiedene Gründe. Erstens ist das Video selbst unvollständig und der Schnitt von Professor Geldsetzer verwirrend, so dass die von uns erwartete, umfassendere und tiefgehendere Darstellung der im Bericht von Herrn Hong aus dem Jahr 2001 erwähnten Themen nicht erfolgt. So wird zum Beispiel der Satz „Hermeneutik verlangt Phantasie", der seinerzeit von Herrn Hong oft zitiert wurde, hier nicht weiter erläutert. Vielmehr ist Hongs Bericht klarer und besser lesbar als der vorliegende unzusammenhängende Text. Zweitens können wir anhand des vorliegenden Textes feststellen, dass es sich weniger um ein geplantes und zielgerichtetes „Interview" als vielmehr um ein improvisiertes, gewissermaßen assoziatives

Alltagsgespräch handelt. Mit anderen Worten: Was wir erwartet haben, war ein ausführliches „Interview" mit dem Philosophen Gadamer, aber was wir bekommen haben, ist ein ganz gewöhnliches Gespräch. Das macht die Lektüre so enttäuschend.

Es lohnt sich jedoch, darüber nachzudenken, wie sich ein echter Dialog formt. Tatsächlich habe ich in den vergangenen Jahren eine ganze Menge von Gadamers Werken gelesen, darunter auch einige Interviews. Was mir an Gadamers Interviews auffällt, ist, dass er sehr zu Abschweifungen neigt und oft von einer Sache zur nächsten geht. Natürlich versuchte der Interviewer, ihn wieder auf das Thema des Gesprächs zu lenken, aber schon bald war er wieder vom Thema abgekommen. Ist dies eine Schwäche oder eine Stärke?

Im vorliegenden Interview erzählt Gadamer, wie er mit seinen Studenten nach den Seminaren in einer nahegelegenen Kneipe etwas trinken ging - eine Form des freien, zwanglosen Austauschs, die seiner Meinung nach nicht durch eine gut geplante Diskussionsrunde ersetzt werden kann. Wir können also sagen, dass für Gadamer das alltägliche improvisierte Gespräch nicht notwendigerweise ein Heideggersches banales „Gerede" darstellt, sondern die Möglichkeit eines echten Dialogs überhaupt erst gibt. Der Grund dafür ist, dass ein Gespräch keine Wissensvermittlung beabsichtigt, sondern eine gegenseitige Inspiration und eine gemeinsame Suche nach der Wahrheit zwischen den Partnern. Wenn wir die richtige Antwort bereits im Voraus festgelegt zu haben glauben und Ideen und Argumente in Form eines Interviews präsentieren, ist dies kein echter Dialog im Sinne Gadamers; der wahre Dialog lehrt keine vorgefertigten Wahrheiten, sondern diese werden im Dialog gesucht. Unter diesem Gesichtspunkt erhält das vorliegende Interview eine positivere Bedeutung. Hier geht es nicht um einen östlichen Gelehrten, der einen Meister der Hermeneutik nach der

Wahrheit fragt, sondern um die Erhellung der Wahrheit in einem gemeinsamen Austausch.

Natürlich ist ein echter Dialog nie völlig unorganisiert, sondern unter der chaotischen Oberfläche liegt ein Leitfaden. Das Hauptthema dieses Dialogs, d.h. die zentrale Frage, um die er sich dreht, ist meines Erachtens die Frage von Herrn Hong: „Ist eine chinesische Hermeneutik möglich und wie sollte sie sich entwickeln?" Wir könnten dies die Frage nach der chinesischen Hermeneutik nennen. Mit dieser Frage im Hinterkopf besuchte Herr Hong Professor Gadamer, und in ihrem Gespräch kamen sie immer wieder auf dieses Thema zurück.

Die Möglichkeit einer chinesischen Hermeneutik ist heute nicht mehr so umstritten. Zu Beginn des 21. Jahrhunderts war sie es jedoch. Die Schlüsselfrage ist hier natürlich nicht, ob sich aus der reichen Tradition der klassischen Auslegung im antiken China Methodiken und Theorien herauskristallisieren lassen, um eine „chinesische (klassische) Hermeneutik" zu bilden, sondern ob die chinesische Hermeneutik international anerkannt werden und am Aufbau und der Entwicklung einer weltweiten hermeneutischen Theorie teilnehmen kann. Viele Wissenschaftler sind auf der ersten Ebene stehen geblieben, was eine sehr sinnvolle Arbeit sein mag, aber nicht ausreicht, um die Frage nach der chinesischen Hermeneutik zu beantworten. So wie die Westler nicht von „westlicher Hermeneutik" sprechen, wenn sie über ihre eigenen hermeneutischen Theorien sprechen (sie verwenden diesen Begriff nur, wenn sie zwischen den hermeneutischen Theorien des Westens und anderer Zivilisationen vergleichen), müssen wir, wenn wir lediglich ein theoretisches System der „klassischen Hermeneutik" konstruieren, auch nicht betonen, dass es sich um „chinesische Hermeneutik" handelt. Der Kern der Frage nach der chinesischen Hermeneutik ist also, *wie die chinesische Hermeneutik in einen Dialog mit der west-*

lichen Hermeneutik treten und in diesem Dialog gemeinsam eine Art universeller hermeneutischer Theorie konstruieren kann.

In dem Gespräch zwischen Herrn Hong und Herrn Gadamer können wir mindestens zwei Antworten auf die von ihm aufgeworfene Frage nach der chinesischen Hermeneutik erkennen. Erstens schätzte Gadamer die chinesische Sprache sehr, insofern er Herrn Hong nicht nur bat, ihm an Ort und Stelle ein altes Gedicht zu rezitieren, sondern sogar vorschlug, dass die Menschen in den nächsten 200 Jahren genauso viel Chinesisch lernen sollten, wie sie heute Englisch lernten. Hinter dem Interesse an der Sprache steht ein Interesse an den Ideen und der Kultur, die sie transportiert. Gadamers Wertschätzung für die chinesische Sprache spiegelt auch die großen Hoffnungen wider, die er in das chinesische Denken setzte. Die gegenwärtige hermeneutische Theorie ist in der Tat eng mit der westlichen Sprache und dem westlichen metaphysischen Denken verbunden. In diesem Sinne erkennt Gadamer mit seiner Aussage die Bedeutung des traditionellen chinesischen Denkens für die künftige Entwicklung der Hermeneutik an, das als Ideenquelle für die Konstruktion einer hermeneutischen Theorie herangezogen werden könne. *Die Kosmopolitisierung der Hermeneutik ist nicht eine Globalisierung der westlichen Hermeneutik, sondern die gemeinsame Darstellung einer universellen Hermeneutik im Dialog zwischen Ost und West.* Im Gespräch wies Gadamer darauf hin, dass im 19. und 20. Jahrhundert die Menschen aus dem Osten stets in die westliche Welt gingen, um vom Westen zu lernen und sich fortgeschrittenes Wissen (einschließlich naturwissenschaftlicher Kenntnisse) anzueignen; in Zukunft werde die Beziehung zwischen dem Osten und dem Westen jedoch nicht mehr ein einseitiger Wissenstransfer von West nach Ost sein, sondern ein gegenseitiges Lernen und eine gemeinsame Förderung des Fortschritts der menschlichen Kultur.

Zweitens geht es uns um eine universelle hermeneutische Theorie, weil wir es alle mit derselben Welt und derselben Zukunft zu tun haben, ob wir nun aus dem Osten oder aus dem Westen kommen. In seinem Interview äußerte Gadamer seine Befürchtungen über das zukünftige Schicksal der Menschheit, über die Möglichkeit ihrer Zerstörung unter der Herrschaft der Technik. Als philosophische Theorie sollte die Hermeneutik eine Grundlage für den Widerstand gegen diese Gefahr liefern. In späteren Jahren verstand Gadamer die Hermeneutik als praktische Philosophie, konkret: als Ethik und Politik. Eine Ethik und Politik im hermeneutischen Sinne würde eine neue Richtung für das gemeinsame zukünftige Schicksal der Menschheit vorgeben. Hier müssen sowohl die Menschen im Osten als auch die im Westen verantwortungsbewusst an diesem kulturellen Aufbau mitwirken, indem sie Gemeinsamkeiten suchen und gleichzeitig die Unterschiede bewahren, anstatt sich zu bekämpfen. In diesem Sinne bedeutet *die Schaffung einer „chinesischen Hermeneutik" ihre Selbstaufhebung, d.h. die Integration in eine universelle Hermeneutik des gemeinsamen Schicksals der Menschheit. Hier wird die Hermeneutik zum Vermittler und zur Brücke zwischen den verschiedenen menschlichen Kulturen.*

Meiner Meinung nach sind diese beiden Punkte die wertvollsten Aspekte dieses Interviews. Durch den Austausch mit Gadamer löste Herr Hong die Frage nach der chinesischen Hermeneutik in seinem Kopf: Wir müssen nicht nur die Bedeutung der chinesischen Hermeneutik für die universelle Hermeneutik anerkennen, sondern auch erkennen, dass die chinesische Hermeneutik erst dann ihre wahre Bedeutung erlangt, wenn sie universal wird.

Es ist anzumerken, dass Gadamer zu Lebzeiten eine Reihe von Interviews gegeben hat, von denen einige veröffentlicht wurden, wie z.B. die Interviews mit Carsten Dutt und Riccardo

Dottori. Das Gadamer-Interview von Herrn Handing Hong hat jedoch seine ganz eigene Bedeutung. Die Bedeutung liegt nicht nur darin, dass es die Zweifel eines chinesischen Hermeneutik-Forschers ausräumte und ihm Vertrauen in seine Forschung verschaffte, sondern auch darin, dass es ein wichtiges Ereignis des Austauschs und Dialogs in der Geschichte der chinesischen und westlichen Hermeneutik war. In dieser Hinsicht hat das Interview eine weitreichende wirkungsgeschichtliche Bedeutung. Natürlich hat Gadamer nur einen Impuls dafür gegeben, während seine Entwicklung und Vollendung von den intellektuellen Bemühungen unserer chinesischen Hermeneutiker abhängt. In den zwanzig Jahren, die seit dem Interview vergangen sind, haben chinesische Hermeneutiker einerseits die westliche Hermeneutik eingehender studiert und andererseits allmählich einen chinesischen Diskurs und einen chinesischen Weg in der Hermeneutik etabliert und die Grundlage für den Austausch und den Dialog zwischen der chinesischen und der westlichen Hermeneutik geschaffen.

Heute, zwanzig Jahre nach dem Interview, können wir einen Blick auf das Interview in seiner ursprünglichen Form werfen, was uns die Gelegenheit bietet, einen Blick auf die nächsten zwanzig Jahre chinesischer hermeneutischer Studien zu werfen. Ich denke, dass sich in den nächsten zwanzig Jahren immer mehr Menschen im Westen für die chinesische Hermeneutik interessieren werden, und sie werden bedauern, dass sie kein Chinesisch können. Gleichzeitig müssen wir die Übersetzung chinesischer hermeneutischer Forschungsergebnisse für den Westen verstärken, um die philosophische Weisheit des Ostens in wichtigen Problemen der menschlichen Gemeinschaft zu verdeutlichen und am Aufbau einer gemeinsamen Wahrheit und eines gemeinsamen Diskurses im Dialog mitzuwirken.

* * *

Zu diesem Zweck wird das vorliegende Buch zusammenge-stellt. Es enthält eine Reihe von Artikeln von Professor Handing Hong, die sich in zwei Teile gliedern lassen. Einer davon sind seine Überlegungen zur Hermeneutik, insbesondere zur Konstruktion der chinesischen Hermeneutik. Der zweite Teil beinhaltet seine erinnernden Aufsätze zu Gadamer, zum einen seine Übersetzung von *Wahrheit und Methode*, zum anderen eine Aufzeichnung seiner beiden Besuche bei Gadamer. Man kann sagen, dass diese Beiträge alle um den Besuch von Professor Hong bei Gadamer in Heidelberg im Jahr 2001 kreisen, der sowohl ein wichtiges Ereignis in der Geschichte des Austauschs zwischen chinesischer und westlicher Hermeneutik als auch ein Wegweiser für Hongs Untersuchungen zur chinesischen Hermeneutik war.

Die Herausgabe dieses Buches erfolgte mit freundlicher Unterstützung von Professor Hong, und der Dank gilt auch den Übersetzern (Wei Chen, Karl Kraatz, Deyuan Huang) und Korrekturlesern (Reinald G. Schrecker für die deutschen Titel und Sally Borthwick für den englischen) der verschiedenen enthaltenen Titel. Schließlich möchte ich dem Verleger Wolfgang Sohst für seine Unterstützung danken. Ich denke, die Veröffentlichung dieses Buches ist ein kleiner Neuanfang im Austausch zwischen chinesischer und westlicher Hermeneutik, und ich hoffe, dass wir in dieser Hinsicht gemeinsam noch große Fortschritte machen werden.

Hongjian Wang

Changsha, 5. März 2023

Neue Überlegungen zur Hermeneutik

Hermeneutik als Kunst der Auslegung und als Philosophieren

Die Hermeneutik ist eine der wichtigsten Strömungen in der zeitgenössischen Philosophie. Sie ist jedoch kein spezifischer Begriff, der eine bestimmte Denkschule definiert; im Allgemeinen werden philosophische Schulen durch einen „-ismus" gekennzeichnet, wie z. B. der Neokantianismus, der Positivismus, der Existentialismus, der Strukturalismus usw., und offensichtlich ist die Hermeneutik kein solcher Ismus oder solche Schule. Ebenso ist die Hermeneutik keine echte logisch aufgebaute Wissenschaft oder Lehre, denn eine echte Wissenschaft oder Lehre würde auf „-ologie" enden, wie z. B. Biologie, Psychologie, Phänomenologie, während die Hermeneutik auf „-ik" endet, wie z. B. Logik, Rhetorik, Dialektik usw. Sie sind keine Namen, die eine bestimmte Theorie oder Doktrin bezeichnen, sondern eher Operationen oder Techniken in einer bestimmten Disziplin oder einem bestimmten Wissensgebiet, so ist die Hermeneutik auch keine bestimmte Theorie oder Doktrin, sondern eine neuartige zeitgenössische Operation der Interpretation. Kurz gesagt, es handelt sich nicht um eine philosophische Theorie, sondern um die Kunst der philosophischen Interpretation. Eine bessere Übersetzung von Hermeneutik wäre daher „Kunst der Auslegung".

In den Enzyklopädien wird die Hermeneutik als die Disziplin betrachtet, die die Regeln der Textauslegung anleitet, freilich sollte es neben der Textauslegung auch eine Auslegung anderer menschlicher Werke (wie Gemälde, Skulpturen, Architektur usw.) und menschlicher Verhaltensweisen geben. Man sollte sagen, dass die Hermeneutik als Kunst der Auslegung (*techne hermeneutike*) von menschlichen Werken, Texten und Verhaltensweisen handelt - was Dilthey als „die Objektivierung des Geistes" und Emilio Betti „sinnhaltige Formen" nennt. Ich will dies jedoch noch erweitern, indem ich sage, dass die Hermeneutik das zeitgenössische *Philosophieren* sei.

Wie kann eine Disziplin der Interpretation der Name für eine Art des Philosophierens sein? Wir können dies sowohl in Bezug auf die Breite als auch auf die Tiefe verstehen. Wenn sich die Hermeneutik in unserer Zeit als philosophische Aktivität etablieren konnte, dann deshalb, weil wir uns der Universalität des Problems der Interpretation im Bereich der Erkenntnis bewusst geworden sind. Im Gegensatz zu den vier Disziplinen, die sich auf rein interpretative Studien beschränkten, wie die Exegese, die Philologie, die Jurisprudenz und die Geschichte, die sich bis zum 19. Jahrhundert mit der Hermeneutik oder der Kunst der Interpretation beschäftigten, taucht die Frage der Interpretation heute als *ursprüngliches universelles Prinzip* allen Wissens auf, d. h. der Raum der Interpretation hat unseren kognitiven Raum fast vollständig ausgefüllt.

Wenn heute jemand sagt, die Tradition der Interpretation sei zwar stark in unserem Erkenntnisraum etabliert, aber das wissenschaftliche und logische Denken jenseits der Interpretation sei noch stärker, dann können wir ihm sagen, dass selbst Erkenntnistheoretiker wie Karl Popper und Wissenschaftshistoriker wie Thomas Kuhn uns längst gelehrt haben, inwiefern wissenschaftliche Theorien immer Interpretationen sind. Ob euklidische oder nicht-euklidische Geometrie, ob Newtonsche Mechanik oder Einsteinsche Relativitätstheorie, ob Atom- oder Quantentheorie, sie alle sind nichts anderes als Interpretationen des Realen in einem bestimmten Rahmen oder unter bestimmten Bedingungen. Die Wissenschaft beschränkt sich nicht auf die Beschreibung von Tatsachen, wie uns die Positivisten und der gesunde Menschenverstand glauben machen wollen; sie muss sie organisieren, sie begrifflich fassen, mit anderen Worten: sie muss sie interpretieren. Die zeitgenössische Erkenntnistheorie zieht hermeneutische Schlussfolgerungen aus Kants Unterscheidung zwischen den Erscheinungen und den Dingen an sich; Wissenschaft ist keine bloße Reflexion über das Reale, wie es ist, sondern muss eine Formatierung, Interpretation und Übersetzung sein, die von den Erscheinungen ausgehen muss.

Andererseits liegt die Hermeneutik als das Philosophieren nicht nur darin, dass die Erkenntnis des Realen in der Interpretation liegt, dass das reale Universum sich aus dem interpretierten Universum ableitet, sondern auch darin, dass das, was die Hermeneutik Interpretation nennt, nicht nur eine objektive Beschreibung des Realen ist, sondern auch eine Veränderung und Transformation des Realen. Die Wiederbelebung des Interpretationskonzepts im 20. Jahrhundert hat zu einer kreativen Revolution dieses Konzepts geführt, bei der alte Dinge zu neuen Bedeutungen entfesselt werden können. Diese revolutionäre Wendung des Interpretationskonzepts begann tatsächlich bereits im 19. Jahrhundert, wenn wir zum Beispiel an Marx' Unterscheidung zwischen Interpretation und Veränderung der Welt und an Nietzsches Unterscheidung zwischen Wahrheit und Interpretation denken.

Diese Breite und Tiefe der interpretativen Dimension im kognitiven Bereich ermöglicht es uns, den wichtigen Platz der Hermeneutik in der heutigen Philosophie zu erkennen. Wenn sich herausstellt, dass alles menschliche Wissen, alle Einstellungen und Verhaltensweisen einer Interpretation des Realen folgen, die auch die Kraft hat, die Welt zu verändern oder zu transformieren, erhält die Hermeneutik eine universelle Verwurzelung. Somit erfüllt die Hermeneutik den Anspruch, philosophisch zu sein, sie wird zur Philosophie. Aristoteles sagte, die Metaphysik sei die erste Philosophie (*prima philosophia*), und wenn wir bedenken, dass die Metaphysik auch eine philosophische Kunst ist, eine Interpretation des Realen von oben und unten (Wesen und Phänomen, Eins und Viele, Gott und die Welt), von links und rechts (Subjekt und Objekt) und von vorne und hinten (Sein und Zeit), dann kann man sagen, dass die Hermeneutik die erste Philosophie sei.

(Übersetzt von Hongjian Wang)

The Sinicization of Hermeneutics

A Universal Conception of Classical Hermeneutics[1]

Abstract: We need to start from the approach to classical annotation of *jingxue* (Confucian classical studies), with its long history and experience, and to make use of the fine resources of contemporary Western hermeneutics, so as to build a universal classical hermeneutics that will bridge Chinese and foreign thought in the past and the present. This is a necessary path to opening up and innovating China's fine traditional culture. To carry out this important academic project of universal classical hermeneutics, it is necessary to gain an in-depth understanding of the developmental history of Western hermeneutics and contemporary philosophical hermeneutics, and especially to fully grasp Gadamer's hermeneutical thought and theories and their contemporary development. In addition, it is necessary to comprehensively organize the vast experience and long history of *jingxue* and its branches, such as exegesis, textual studies, philology, bibliography and hermeneutics, and to take the modernization of *jingxue* as a starting point for establishing a type of universal classical hermeneutics that is different from traditional Chinese *jingxue* but also superior to Western hermeneutics. Only in this way can we base ourselves on China, learn from foreign countries, excavate history and grasp the contemporary, so as to fully reflect the "Chinese style and manner" and characteristics in disciplinary, academic and discourse systems.

Philosophical circles in China are currently faced with two important types of interpretation of the classics: Western hermeneutics and Chinese study of the Confucian classics. Western hermeneutics involves not only the hermeneutics of philosophy, but also the hermeneutics of literature, history, law,

---

1   This article was first published in *Social Sciences in China* (Chinese Edition), 2020, no. 1.

theology, art, and so forth. Corresponding to the Western hermeneutic tradition is the Chinese study of the Confucian classics, a traditional humanist discipline that is similar to Western hermeneutics. Developing modern classical hermeneutics from the traditional study of the Confucian classics is an innovative task of transformation for contemporary philosophy in the Chinese language.

I.

A Comparison of Confucian Classical Learning and Western Hermeneutics

Modernizing the study of the Confucian classics is a tricky issue for Chinese scholars today. Previously there were two different approaches: one, termed "new classical learning," took the basic path of throwing off Western conceptual frameworks and language and restoring the vitality of traditional Chinese culture. This involved sorting through the existing practice and experience of Chinese study of the Confucian classics and using concepts and language that were indigenous to China. The other, the hermeneutic approach, proposed developing a hermeneutics of the classics with Chinese characteristics that merges with but differs from Western hermeneutics; this entailed critical absorption of Western hermeneutics on the basis of the wealth of traditional interpretations of the Chinese classics. We propose the latter, i.e., the hermeneutic approach, in the sense of a modernized philosophy proper to China that is based on critical dialogue with the traditional Chinese classics in the new and higher sphere of world philosophy. To this end, we propose a transition from China's study or interpretation of the Confucian classics to "Chinese classical hermeneutics." On the one

18

hand, this affirms our longstanding tradition of interpretation of the classics and the rich hermeneutic experience it reflects; on the other, it suggests that the proposed "Chinese classical hermeneutics" should be a kind of classical hermeneutics that is universal in nature and that different both from traditional study of the Confucian classics and general Western theories of hermeneutics.

Confucianism is the mainstream of traditional Chinese culture, and study of the Confucian classics lies at the heart of Confucianism. Classical learning could be said to mean the annotation and interpretation of the classics. A comprehensive survey of China's Confucian learning reveals several characteristics relevant to hermeneutics, listed below. Firstly, this scholarship consists not only of interpretations of the Confucian classics (including the various classical commentaries, annotations, etc.: *zhuan* 传, *zhu* 注, *shu* 疏 and *jie* 解), but also of the learning and techniques employed in carrying out this task. This involves not only a method but a philosophy, imbued not only with heavenly principles and the mind of man but also with inner sagehood and outer kingship. Secondly, it is a form of knowledge in the broadest sense, one that differs from but includes literature, history, philosophy, economics, politics, and ethics. Philosophically, it not only encompasses Chinese philosophy, but also serves as the philosophical basis of other disciplines. Third, it has its own developmental history and schools of thought, ranging from the Western Han New Text School (*jinwen jingxue* 今文经学), the Eastern Han Old Text School (*guwenjingxue* 古文经学), Sui and Tang interpretations of earlier exegesis (*elucidation of the classics* 义疏经学), the Song, Yuan and Ming School of Song learning (*songxue jingxue* 宋学经学), the Qing return to Han dynasty classical learning via textual analysis (*hanxue jingxue* 汉学经学), and the late Qing integration of the Old and New Text schools (*jin-guwen jingxue* 今古文经学). And lastly, and most importantly, it is an intermediary between the past and present and the traditional and the modern, an intermediary with some two thousand years of scholarly history.

Western hermeneutics would seem to have similarities with the four points above. First, hermeneutics is not only concerned with understanding and interpretation, but also with classical interpretation; nor does it concern simply the ontology of understanding and interpretation, but also the associated methodology. As far as the actual interpretation of classical texts is concerned, we know that Schleiermacher translated Plato, Heidegger interpreted Aristotle and Gadamer produced interpretations of Plato, etc. Second, in a sense hermeneutics is philosophy, that is, philosophical hermeneutics, but we also have the hermeneutics of literature, history, law, theology and art, for all of which hermeneutics furnishes a philosophical basis. Third, in terms of time, we have ancient, initial modern (late Qing/Republican) and contemporary hermeneutics, and in terms of contents and levels, we have methodological and ontological hermeneutics. Fourth, Western hermeneutics likewise functions as an intermediary between the past and present and the traditional and the modern.

Therefore, whether it is a matter of Sinicizing Western hermeneutics or modernizing and globalizing Chinese philosophy, it would seem that Chinese work on the Confucian classics offers a way forward. This field has basic characteristics of its own that constitute an asset of inestimable significance in the Chinese construction of a universal classical hermeneutics.

First, ever since Confucius said "I transmit the bequeathed teaching without inventing anything of my own. I trust and love the past," Chinese scholarship started on a path of classical interpretation that gave rise to the age-old tradition of interpretation of the Confucian classics. In terms of its duration and the number of works it produced, one could say that the tradition of classical interpretation was far more important in China than in the West. Such interpretation had a rigorous three-layer structure composed of *jing* 经 (classics), *zhuan* 传 (commentary), and *zhu* 注 (annotations). The classics were central; *zhuan* and *ji* 记 (records) were auxiliaries, and *zhujie* 注解 (annotation), *zhangju* 章句 (explanations at the level of words or sentences) and *yishu* 义疏 (elucidation) provide the finishing touches. Yang Quan, a native of the Kingdom of Wu during the Three Kingdoms period, put it metaphorically: "The Five Classics are the sea; the *zhuan* and the *ji* are the four large rivers; and the other [pre-Qin] philosophers are lesser rivers." Zhangsun Wuji, of the early Tang dynasty, remarked, "What was written by the sages of the past is termed classics; the interpretations contributed by *zhuanshi* 传师 (masters of *zhuan*) are called commentaries, as in the Zuo Qiuming's commentary on the *Spring and Autumn Annals* and the Zixia's commentary on the *Book of Rites*; and in recent times, the annotation and explanation of the classics has been termed elucidation."[2] Of course, this structure has undergone certain changes. Specifically, pre-Qin Confucianism and the classical learning of the Western and Eastern Han and Six Dynasties periods all revolved around the sorting out, compilation, narration and annotation of the Six Classics, but after the mid-Tang period, the focus of interpretation of the Confucian classics had shifted from the classics to commentaries and records (*zhuanji*), and by the Southern Song a system centered on the Four Books and the *Commentary on the Book of Changes* had finally emerged.

Second, Confucian learning not only laid down a unique three-layer classical structure made up of the classics, commen-

---

2 Quoted from Jing Haifeng, *The Modern Interpretation of Chinese Philosophy*, p. 34.

taries and annotations, but also had a unique methodological approach that included *xungu* 训沽 (philology), *kaozheng* 考证 (evidential learning), *wenzi* 文字 (study of ancient characters), and *yinyun* 音韵 (study of phonology and rhymes). How was it that Chinese interpretation of the classics came to stress the probing of texts and words and their literal meaning? According to the *Records of the Grand Historian: The Hereditary House of Confucius*, "At the time of Confucius, the house of Zhou was in decline, ritual and music had been abandoned, and the *Book of Songs* and the *Book of History* were imperfect. Confucius traced the rites back to the Three Dynasties (Xia, Shang and Zhou), compiled the *Book of History*, and recorded events as long ago as Yao and Shun and as recent as Duke Mu of Qin. He said, 'I can speak of the rites of Xia, but there is not enough evidence for the state of Qi; I can speak of the rites of Shang, but there is not enough evidence for the state of Song. If there were enough, I could demonstrate it. '"[3] This shows that an important reason for the emphasis on the explanations of ancient words in the interpretation of the Confucian classics is that the classic texts, both partially and as a whole, had undergone a historical sea change, and thus could not be fully grasped by later generations. This situation is similar to the emergence of early modern Western *Philologie*, the precursor of *klassische Altertumswissenschaften*. Over the course of its long history of interpretation of the Confucian classics, Chinese classical learning developed a variety of interpretive methods and trends, including philological studies of ancient words and interpretations of meanings and principles; interpretations in the style of *hanxue* (Han learning) and *songxue* (Song learning) or in the vein of "I annotate the Six Classics and the Six Classics annotate me," etc. This indi-

---

3 Sima Qian, *Records of the Grand Historian: Hereditary House of Confucius*, pp. 1935- 1936.

cates the very high theoretical level reached by China's tradition of classical interpretation. Throughout successive dynasties, the annotation of the classics has produced particular techniques of classical interpretation that provide a summing up of language, history and psychology. With language, interpretive methods include "creating images to exhaust meanings," "using names to present what is real," "distinguishing between names to analyze principles," "casting off the words once the meaning is grasped," and "seeking meaning through sounds"; with history, interpretive methods include "using the classics to elucidate events," "knowing people; speaking of the world," and revealing "great meaning through subtle words"; and with psychology, interpretive methods include "using one's mind to understand the work of another," "learning through personal commitment,"[4] and so on. Further, some scholars have concluded that there are three routes for the interpretation of the Confucian classics: Mencius's method, "using one's mind to understand the work of another," is an appeal to the personal life experience of the interpreter of the classics; one could call it the Confucian hermeneutics of the philosophy of human nature and the mind. The second method that takes the ideal of governing the country and relieving the suffering of the people as the goal of interpretation; one could call this the Confucian hermeneutics of political science. Finally, there is the method that clarifies the historical significance of the classics through explanations of ancient words, or Confucian hermeneutics as philology.

Third, Chinese classical interpretation has always taken the path of practice rather than pure theory. Confucian classical learning stresses practical statecraft (*jing shi zhi yong* 经世致用) . The Qing scholar Fang Bao said in "Chuan Xin Lu Xu 传信录序,"

---

4 Zhou Guangqing, *Introduction to Chinese Classical Hermeneutics*, pp. 11- 12.

"In ancient times people called scholars were clear in their minds on exhausting the principles of things and relieving the suffering of the people. What cannot be used should not be studied." The term *jingshi* 经世 can also be referred to as *jing lun* 经纶.[5] Zhu Xi explains in his *Annotations on the Doctrine of the Mean (Zhongyong Zhangju* 中庸章句*)*, "*Jing* 经 and *lun* 纶 are both items in the silk industry. *Jing* means to tidy up and separate angled threads, while *lun* means to integrate them according to their types. ... The virtue of the sage is utmost sincerity without arrogance. Therefore, he is able to behave exactly in accord with ethics, setting a good example for all later generations. That is how the expression *jinglun* came into being. "[6] Another example is Confucius' answers to his disciples questions about human-heartedness or benevolence in the *Analects*; all his replies refer to the specific situations of different people, rather than providing an eternal and unchanging response. His responses are in sharp contrast with Socrates' answer to the question of what virtue, justice, and courage are. Socrates seeks to identify commonalities and differences and develops logical arguments on the basis of genus and difference (*per genus et differentiam*), whereas Confucius does not frame his replies using logic, but rather offers specific practical guidance adapted to each situation (*jeweilige*). This is more in line with the practical wisdom of hermeneutics. Therefore, we must realize that over the long course of Confucian classical interpretation, Chinese scholars have developed a way of understanding the classics that is different from that of Western classical hermeneutics. The latter tends to be based on the dichotomy of subject and object and adopts an objective epistemological interpretation that is external and neutral and avoids the infiltration of the subjective as much as possible. As

---

5   Feng Tianyu, *The Spirit of Confucian Classics*, p. 260.

6   Zhu Xi, *Si Shu Zhang Ju Jizhu*, p. 38.

Gadamer said in his critique of the romantic followers of hermeneutics, they equate understanding with interpretation but forget application. Therefore, they understand and interpret texts like scientists studying something in a laboratory, attempting an objective and neutral understanding without the interference of the interpreters themselves. Conversely, in Chinese classical hermeneutics, understanding the classics is not simply a matter of methodology, but of one's moral edification and the cultivation of virtue. "The way of the sage is heard with the ear, kept in the heart, accumulated as virtuous acts, and acted on as an enterprise. If they look only at the level of the words, they are inferior."[7] In comparison with Western classical hermeneutics, Chinese interpreters of classics pay more attention to the cultivation of morality and virtue through practice. They state that "The scholars of ancient times worked to cultivate themselves, hoping to achieve cultivation within themselves, but the scholars of today are cultivating themselves for others, with a view to having their learning recognized." They claim that the way of learning is the "approach to sagehood," and say that "benevolence is to be found in earnest inquiry and thinking about what is near at hand."[8]

The three points above give the most important features of classical learning or classical interpretation that are comparable to Western hermeneutics. Of course, we also need to see the difference between the two. Here we must first clarify two concepts, namely, *jingdian* 经典 (classics, *classicus*, or *Klassik*) and *shengdian* 圣典 (the classics or the *Kanon*). In the ancient West, the *classicus* and the canon were related. The latter is a term in Western theology referring to sacred texts that have a quasi-religious or authoritative status. "Sacred" means that the text is

---

7   Zhou Dunyi, *Zhou Zi Tong Shu*, p. 41.

8   Zhu Xi, *Jin Si Lu*, pp. 54, 67.

the subject of faith, not of inquiry: it rejects any pluralist interpretation. Conversely, *classicus* as a term in Western philosophy refers above all to the subject of inquiry and understanding, not the subject of belief; as its meaning is repeatedly interpreted by us, *classicus* does not stand for any absolute truth. Given that philosophy was closely connected with theology in the early West, the *classicus* became sacred scripture, so what then prevailed was mainly dogmatic hermeneutics. However, with the development of modern science and civilization, the hermeneutics of modern Western has developed a hermeneutics of inquiry or zetetic hermeneutics. Whereas dogmatic hermeneutics aims at finding fixed meanings that are already well-known from outstanding texts and applying them as instructive truths and guidance to specific current situations, zetetic hermeneutics, by contrast, does not search for immutable fixed meanings in the text, but rather explores the constantly renewed and infinite tension of lived experience in all texts. Dogmatic hermeneutics can be termed exegesis.

Historically, classical interpretation in the ancient West had two forms of hermeneutics: theological hermeneutics and jurisprudential hermeneutics. The former interpreted the Bible, while the latter interpreted Roman law. Both fall under the dogmatic hermeneutics that constituted the early developmental form of Western hermeneutics. It was from this tradition of classical interpretation that early Western philosophy began, and into medieval times theologians such as Augustine and Aquinas expounded the interpretation of the classics, as in Aquinas's *Commentary on Aristotle's Metaphysics*. The first Western work to have hermeneutics in the title was Johann Conrad Dannhauer's *Sacred Hermeneutics*. This originally represented a fine tradition, with the method of classical interpretation serving to advance both theology and philosophy.[9] However, around the 18th century, British empiricism, French rationalism, and German critical philosophy did not pursue this line of inquiry. Philosophers wrote their own philosophies, such as Hume's *An Enquiry concerning Human Understanding*, Descartes' *Meditations*, and Kant's *Critique of Pure Reason*. None of these works takes the form of interpretation of the classics; rather, they are all independent philosophical writings. Although much of their thought came from the classics, they did not wish to confine themselves to the work of annotation; they wanted to have something of their own and construct their own philosophies. Therefore, this period marked the start of the Western philosophical tradition's divergence from that of ancient and medieval times. Whence came this transformation? It arose from the development of the zetetic form of hermeneutics—a kind of philological or universal hermeneutics that was quite different from the ancient theological and jurisprudential hermeneutics. Although the object of study was still the classics, the classics were no longer canonical texts; they were the object not of faith, but of epistemology. In a word, exegesis, that is, dogmatic hermeneutics, was abandoned, and the modern zetetic hermeneutics was developed.[10]

---

9 Historically and in terms of experience, classical commentaries in the ancient West number, for Aristotle alone, about three hundred, including those by Alexander of Aphrodisias, Philoponus, Porphyry and Simplicius, which come respectively from the Byzantine, Islamic, medieval and Renaissance eras. From 1987 to 2012, King's College, London, published over a hundred volumes of *Ancient Commentators on Aristotle*; and Richard Sorabji subsequently edited a series of *Commentaria in Aristotelem Graeca* (CAG). There are, in addition, some further collections of studies of ancient commentaries on Aristotle, such as *The Philosophy of the Commentators, 200-600 AD; Aristotle Transformed: The Ancient Commentators and Their Influence; Philosophy, Science & Exegesis: In Greek, Arabic & Latin Commentaries: Greek and Roman Philosophy 100 B.C-200 A.D.*, etc.

10 Certainly, from the early years of the modern West on, classical interpretation did not disappear, but rather existed in divergent forms. In

Historically, we can discuss the change in Western interpretation of the classics in terms of the difference between *"jingdian* 经典*"* and *"gudian* 古典*."* As far as the concept of *jingdian* is concerned, Chinese and European languages are very different. *"Klassik"* (classic) can be translated into Chinese as either *jingdian* or *gudian*, but in the West, both in English and German, the one word *"Klassik"* (classic) covers both *gudian* and *jingdian*. If we know a little about the history of concepts, we will see that this involves an intricate process of change. *Klassik* or classic generally has three layers of meaning in both China and the West: 1) As a historical concept, it refers to writings handed down from classical antiquity. The *jing* or Confucian classics of today's classical learning (*jingxue*) or classical writings (*jingdian*) are simply the Six Classics or Thirteen Classics of ancient times, and the same is true in the West, where the word generally refers to works from ancient Greece or Rome. *Jingdian* is thus a historical concept bound up with antiquity. 2) It is also a concept

early modern German philosophy, for example, we can distinguish three traditions of classical interpretation. One is the classical interpretation undertaken in critical philosophy and German idealism, that is, the tradition running from Kant to Hegel and Schelling. Ancient Greek philosophy was revived in Germany and amalgamated with native German thought through Kant's explanation of Plato's theory of ideas, Hegel's interpretation of ancient Greek philosophy, and Schelling's commentary on *Timaeus*, which defined the nature of German philosophy. Another was the Romantic tradition of Schleiermacher and Schlegel. Schleiermacher's universal hermeneutics derived from theological and jurisprudential hermeneutics but gave German classical interpretation a form that differed from that of philosophical interpretation: the hermeneutics of classical interpretation, as in Schleiermacher's exposition of Plato in the course of translating the philosopher's complete works and Schlegel's annotations to the history of Greece, also reflect a new interpretative tendency, that of emphasizing the author's original intention. And finally, the last of the traditions of classical interpretation was the school of historical philology first developed by Friedrich August Wolf and August Beck [Böckh]; the latter is best known for his *Enzyklopädie und Methodologie der philologischen Wissenschaften*.

relating to style, i.e., the classical. In the post-Renaissance West, a distinction—one of artistic style—arose between classicism, romanticism, and neoclassicism. In China, too, this distinction is very clear. For example, Peking opera, being classical, differs from modern opera, and the Ming and Qing- type furniture we often see is likewise furniture in the classical style. Thus *jingdian* refers to a style. 3) It is also a normative value concept, representing a model or exemplar (*dianfan* 典范). Today, this is one of the most important meanings of *jingdian*. However, *jingdian* in this sense has completely different meanings in China and the West. *Jingdian* as a norm has always existed in China; here *jingdian* means a constant principle, the constant Way, immutable laws, or "the constant principle of Heaven and Earth; the fitting connection of past and present." Classics do not belong only to antiquity, but to the present. But things are different in the West. *Klassik* (classic) originally only meant "ancient"; it was not until the second century A.D. that a movement in Italian schools made the content of classroom instruction in the classics the supreme model, so that the adjective *classicus* (classical) came to describe the "exemplary" character of the ancient Greek and Roman writers. However, this change in meaning seemed to be unacceptable to the early modern West. The spirit of the times wedded the classical and the ancient; for example, the phrase *die klassische Philosophie* (classical philosophy) was used to refer to ancient (classical) philosophy only. That forced "*jingdian*" into historicity, which implied that it was outdated and had gone downhill, and been replaced by something better. Therefore, wherever *Klassischen* (classics) and *Klassikern* (classical writers) are mentioned in the West today, they are entangled with the topic of "the dispute between ancient and modern." When recalling the protesters of the *Sturm und Drang* era, people oppose the romanticism of German classicism, and mock all types of neoclassicism. Moreover, they know that the contemporary physics represented by the theory of relativity offers more and better things than the classical physics of Galileo and Newton, even though the latter still deserves respect.

China's millennial tradition of Confucian learning cannot identify with this Western tendency. In Chinese culture, what is termed *jingdian* primarily refers to the constant principle or constant Way of Heaven and Earth. Confucius stated long ago "I transmit the bequeathed teaching without inventing anything of my own (*shu er bu zuo*)." "I trust and love the past." "To invent something of my own" is the business of the sage; we can at best "transmit" such ideas. To transmit the bequeathed teaching means to interpret, annotate or explain it.[11] Why was it that Chinese philosophy, very early on, began to "transmit" rather than introduce new ideas? This is related to what the Chinese classics term "the Way of Yao and Shun." According to Confucian classical learning, the Way of Yao and Shun could only be passed on by "seeing" and "hearing" until Confucius drew up the Six Classics, but thereafter it took on a fixed textual form: to study the Six Classics was to understand the Way of Yao and Shun. In the view of classical scholars, the fact that Confucius and his seventy-two disciples have died means that the Confucian classics can be explored but never absolutely grasped. As was said, "The *Book of Songs* has no universal interpretation, the *Book of Changes* displays no unchangeable divination, and the *Spring and Autumn Annals* has no uniform explanation. All follow changes and meanings, but have a single principle: to attend to Heaven."[12] Therefore, the Chinese interpretation of the

---

11 According to the recent research of Professor Yang Naiqiao of Fudan University, *shu* (述) means "follow the bequeathed teaching." See Yang Naiqiao, ed., *China's Classical Confucian Hermeneutics and Western Hermeneutics*, p. 55.

12 Dong Zhongshu, *Chunqiu Fanlu*, p. 775.

classics tended to aim at discovering "great meaning in subtle words," and all of Confucius' editing of the *Book of Songs*, the *Book of History*, the *Book of Rites*, and the *Book of Music* involved interpreting the classics. Since the classics were the work of the sages, they were sacred books, "The classics are nothing other than the universal principles of all under Heaven." Since the "classics" determined by the sages had been confirmed as "the universal principles of all under Heaven," what remained to be done was simply their "annotation and interpretation." From then on, developing philosophical thought by means of interpretation of the classics became an established tradition, i.e., Confucian classical learning. At the outset, we settled on the Five Classics, the Six Classics, and the Thirteen Classics; subsequent developments were simply a process of annotation and interpretation. Many later philosophers expressed their philosophical thoughts in this way. For example, Wang Bi of the Wei and Jin dynasties wrote the *Zhouyi Zhu* 周易注 (*Commentary on the Book of Changes*) and the *Laozi Zhu* 老子注 (*Commentary on the Laozi*) and Guo Xiang wrote the *Zhuangzi Zhu* 庄子注 (*Commentary on the Zhuangzi*); both expressed their philosophical ideas through annotation and interpretation. This is true even of a great figure like Zhu Xi, who wrote *Collected Commentaries on the Four Books*. Of course, we also have some of his sayings, but they were put together by later hands. This tradition continued into the Qing, when Dai Zhen wrote the *Mengzi Ziyi Shuzheng* 孟子字义疏证 (*Commentary on the Meaning of Terms in the Mencius*). Chinese philosophers have generally relied on commentaries on the classics to develop their ideas. We can understand this complexity and multi-directionality as the inevitable result of the canonization (*Kanonization*) of classical interpretation. This canonization was dominated by the consciousness of classical learning, a consciousness primarily expressed in the fact that all interpreters of the classics subscribed to one scholarly mission, that is, to the ideal of inner sagehood and outer kingship. A signer presentative expression of this ideal was the idea of "developing a living principle for Heaven and Earth, setting up a pathway for human beings, retrieving the lost learning of previous sages, and securing peace for all future generations." This consciousness regarded the Confucian classics as an absolute authority, emphasizing "trusting and loving the past," "I follow Zhou," "When speaking, he always made laudatory references to Yao and Shun," and "In action, one must necessarily imitate the Three Dynasties." This tended to lead to an attitude of "venerating and restoring the ancient." Although some scholars of the Confucian classics proposed the mutability of the classics, suggesting "the Six Classics can all be regarded as histories," this exerted little influence upon the entire Chinese tradition of Confucian classical learning.

We can thus see that there are two major differences between modern Western hermeneutics and the traditional study of the Confucian classics in China. Firstly, in modern Western classical interpretation, the layer of "belief" is unimportant. What matters is the spirit of inquiry, that is, the classics are supposed to be applied to our current lives and interpreted in today's context, and to encourage people to become enlightened. Therefore, they do not consider the classics immutable, but believe that the interpretation of each classic can be different in different periods. A very important concept in classical hermeneutics is "the classical." What, then, is "the classical"? Gadamer defined it in his article "Bach und Weimar," saying, "According to a statement of Hegel's, which itself can be considered classical, *classical* means 'that which signifies itself and thereby also interprets itself (*das sich selbst Bedeutende und damit auch sich selber Deutende*). '…Rather, this is a judgment on the inexhaustible riches with which a work or a master enters into the process of historical change."[13] Classics are not static, but ceaselessly renewed; they constantly enable us to win the newest contemporary things. The normative value of the classical is that it is the source of constantly tested truth and life. The historical process of preservation (*Bewahrung*) that, through constantly proving itself (*Bewährung*), allows something true (*ein Wahres*) to come into being. The classical is simply what has been tested through different times and kept its truths. The classical is not existing, but alive; it is not a dead thing that exists outside of us and can only be perceived and assessed by us, but a power that lives within us and becomes one with us. On this point, modern Western hermeneutics differs from China's studies of the Confucian classics.

Secondly, what modern Western hermeneutics seeks to interpret is not the original meaning or intention of the writer of the classic, but the truth within the classic itself. As an essential link in hermeneutics, "understanding" always encompasses the dimension of self- reflection. It is not the simple reduplication of a certain knowledge, but reacquaintance in the new era with what was already known. For this reason, the question of hermeneutics does not arise as long as what is involved is the pure acceptance or exact duplication of a certain mental tradition. Gadamer said, "We are always hearing—listening *to* something and extracting [*sic*] *from* other things. We are *interpreting* in seeing, hearing, receiving. In seeking, we are looking*for* something; we are just not like photographs that reflect everything visible. A real photographer, for instance, is looking for the moment in which the shot would be an interpretation of the experience. So it is obvious that there is a real primacy of interpretation."[14] Ac-

---

13 Hans-Georg Gadamer, *Gesammelte Werke 9*, p. 144.

14 Hans- Georg Gadamer, "The Hermeneutics of Suspicion," in Gary Shapiro and Alan Sica, eds., *Hermeneutics Questions and Prospects*, pp. 59-

cording to the contemporary position of hermeneutics, expressing what is expressed in the process of expression is not only what is to be expressed in the expression, that is, what it refers to, but primarily what is not to be expressed but has actually been expressed together in words and views, i.e., what can almost be said to be "revealed" by the expression. Interpretation here does not refer to the intended meaning, but the meaning that is hidden and must be revealed. Gadamer took Aristotle and Hegel's studies of the history of philosophy as a model. He said that what a philosopher looks for in the philosophers of past times is a certain "idea" rather than what the philosopher himself was in the past and would be in future, and the expression of this idea is what this philosopher is at present. It is precisely this that is the most direct approach to the awakening of those who have died: gaining a grasp of those who have died as if they were still alive. It was in this way that Hegel advanced the history of philosophy. Wherever it may be, as long as there is a philosopher who intends to argue with a particular predecessor, he will endeavor, amid the multiplicity of theories, to grasp something that is single and the same, so that he can establish himself or critically highlight himself in reference to this fixed object (*Gegenbild*). Aristotle, as the first to discover that the history of philosophy was the business of philosophy itself, employed his survey of this history in the critical preparation of his own theories. The result of philosophy's interest in the practical application of its own history has been that all great philosophers, illumined by tradition, had the character of intrinsic greatness, while the development of their theories stayed to some extent in the dark.[15]

60.

15 Hans-Georg Gadamer, *Gesammelte Werke 5*, p. 286.

II.

A Universal Conception of Classical Hermeneutics

The contemporary mainstream Western discipline of philosophical hermeneutics was not introduced into China until the end of the 1970s, but thanks to its vitality it made great progress in a short space of time. As a discipline concerned with understanding and interpretation, it found the drive for further development in China's indigenous tradition of classical interpretation; the combination of Western hermeneutics with this tradition gave rise to an academic movement in China. Many researchers working on the history of Chinese philosophy hope to conduct new research using the methodology of Western hermeneutics, while many researchers in the field of Western hermeneutics expect in turn to develop basic hermeneutic theory by learning from the long tradition and experience of Chinese classical interpretation. But in what direction should this mutually supplementary development proceed?

Here I would like to propose a universal conception of the hermeneutics of classics. Goethe proposed this idea on January 31, 1827: "National literature is now rather an unmeaning term; the epoch of world literature (*Weltlituratur*) is at hand, and every one must strive to hasten its approach."[16] He also said, "the Chinamen think, act, and feel almost exactly like us; and we soon find that we are perfectly like them, excepting that all they do is more clear, more pure, and decorous than with us,"[17] and "We Germans are very likely to fall too easily into this pedantic conceit, when we do not look beyond the narrow circle which surrounds us. I therefore like to look about me in for-

---

16 J.P. Eckermann, *Conversations with Goethe*, p. 213.

17 *Ibid.*, p. 211.

35

eign nations, and advise everyone to do the same."[18] If literature is advancing toward world literature, how much more should philosophy advance towards world philosophy?

First, a brief discussion of the term *jingdian quanshixue* 经典诠释学 (classical hermeneutics). Among foreign scholars, this Chinese term may arouse different ideas. How, then, can it be translated? Can it be translated into German as *die klassische Hermeneutik* or the English "classical hermeneutics?" But there is already a fixed translation for this German or English phrase: *gudian quanshixue* 古典诠释学, rather than *jingdian quanshixue*, just as *die klassische Philosophie* (classical philosophy) is *gudian zhexue* 古典哲学 in Chinese. In Western philosophy, this refers to ancient philosophy, which, with early modern and contemporary philosophy, constitutes the three different stages of philosophy. *Hermeneutik der Klassik* (classic hermeneutics) does not work either, for the word *Klassik* (classic) is a universal abstract concept that can also refer to classical culture, so such a translation would find it hard to convey the idea of *jingdian quanshixue* and could sound very strange to a speaker of German or English. *Jingdian* in the term *jingdian quanshixue* should refer to the hermeneutics of the classics: in German, *Klassikerwerken*, but of course the latter refers not only to writings, but also to works of art such as paintings, sculptures and architecture. As a universal branch of learning concerned with the humanities and social sciences, hermeneutics offers an explanation for human behavior, beliefs, concepts, works (art, architecture, sculpture, painting, etc.) and texts. In other words, hermeneutics is not only the interpretation of past documents and texts, but also the understanding of the entire inner life of others. Wilhelm Dilthey said, "Understanding is what we call this process by which an inside is conferred on a complex of external sensory signs," "*Such*

---

18 *Ibid.*, pp. 363-364.

rule-guided understanding offixed and relatively permanent objecti-fications of life is what we call exegesis or interpretation."[19] "Signs" are here used in the broad sense of the word, referring to human behaviors, beliefs, ideas, works, and texts, which Dilthey calls "objectification of mind," and Emilio Betti calls "the meaningful form." Hermeneutics is thus a branch of learning with a very broad range; it cannot be denied that at present it is one of the most extensive of the human sciences—the humanities and social sciences.

For the fundamental basis of the establishment of a universal classical hermeneutics, I would like to quote a passage from Gadamer's "Introduction" to his *Truth and Method*. It says, "It is part of the elementary experience of philosophy that when we try to understand the classics of philosophical thought, they of themselves make a claim to truth that the consciousness of later times can neither reject nor transcend. The naive self-esteem of the present moment may rebel against the idea that philosophical consciousness admits the possibility that one's own philosophical insight may be inferior to that of Plato or Aristotle, Leibniz, Kant, or Hegel. One might think it a weakness that contemporary philosophy tries to interpret and assimilate its classical heritage with this acknowledgment of its own weakness. But it is undoubtedly a far greater weakness for philosophical thinking not to face such self- examination but to play at being Faust. It is clear that in understanding the texts of these great thinkers, a truth is known that could not be attained in any other way, even if this contradicts the yardstick of research and progress by which science measures itself."[20] Here we can see clearly why philosophy means interpretation of the classics and wherein lies the meaning of interpretation of the classics as philosophy.

---

19 Wilhelm Dilthey, "The Rise of Hermeneutics," pp. 76-77.

20 Hans- Georg Gadamer, *Truth and Method: The Basic Characteristics of Philosophical Hermeneutics*, vol. 1, pp. 4-5.

The following is our conception of the worldwide hermeneutics of the classics.

Firstly, the classical hermeneutics we are talking about should adopt a universal and extensive conception. On the one hand, it refers to global classical hermeneutics, which, as a philosophy, should have a universal character. Philosophy should not be divided into Chinese and foreign; the philosophy of each nation differs only in its form of expression. Analytical philosophy and phenomenology are merely two different philosophical approaches; they do not represent different national philosophies. Classical hermeneutics can be said to represent another viewpoint on and attitude to philosophy. This viewpoint and attitude sees any particular philosophical view or theory as short-lived; only the path of philosophy as classical interpretation will live on forever. On the other hand, "classics" refers not only to Confucian classics, but also to Taoist and Buddhist classics; not only to the classics of Chinese philosophy, but also to those of ancient Greece, Germany, etc.; and not only to classics of philosophy, but also to classics in the fields of literature, history, and religion. In this sense, the wide-ranging hermeneutics of the classics is a part of the humanities and social sciences. We Chinese scholars, whether engaged in Western or Chinese philosophy, literature or history, can all conduct research in the hermeneutics of the classics; this enables us to participate in world philosophy and join the ranks of the humane sciences.

Secondly, when we say "the hermeneutics of the classics," this does not mean that we only study the theories and methods of classical interpretation; we must also interpret the classics themselves. The former is a reflection on the activities of classical interpretation, while the latter is actually equivalent to philosophical research. What we call "hermeneutics" (*Hermeneutik; quanshixue*) looks, in the Chinese, like a branch of learning; it is an interpretive operation. For example, China's traditional interpretation of the classics involved not only the study of theories and methods, but also the interpretation of the classics of philosophy, i.e., research into Chinese philosophy. Moreover, I would like to emphasize that Chinese scholars can also participate in such research on Western philosophy, and their works on Western philosophy will likewise fall into this field. Universal classical hermeneutics will thus put an end to the strange phenomenon of the longstanding division between Chinese and Western philosophy and Chinese and Western literature.

Thirdly, classical hermeneutics is a new form of philosophy. It has achieved a consensus as a common horizon in the global philosophical dialogue, a consensus on studying philosophy at the world's highest and most broad-ranging philosophical level. Classical hermeneutics essentially contains a dimension of self-reflection at the highest level. Universal classical hermeneutics does away with the canonization of Confucian learning as dogmatic hermeneutics, and takes the never-ending path of zetetic hermeneutics in which the classics will be forever be interpreted and the truth will always be open. This is no longer the simplistic acceptance or exact duplication of a particular spiritual tradition, but rather a synthesis or mediation between the past and the present, between strangeness and familiarity, and between tradition and modernity. Gadamer said, "Hermeneutics can be defined as the attempt to overcome this distance in areas where empathy was hard and agreement not easily reached. There is always a gap that must be bridged. Thus, hermeneutics acquires a central place in viewing human experience."[21] Gadamer called this bridging action *Aneignung* (participation or appropriation), claiming that "Participation is a strange word. Its dialectic consists of the fact that participation is not taking

---

21 Hans-Georg Gadamer, "The Hermeneutics of Suspicion," p. 57.

parts, but in a way taking the whole. Everybody who participates in something does not take something away, so that the others cannot have it. The opposite is true: by sharing, by our participating in the things in which we are participating, we enrich them; they do not become smaller, but larger. The whole life of tradition consists exactly in this enrichment so that life is our culture and our past: the whole inner store of our lives is always extending by participating."[22] In short, participation (appropriation) means sharing, and sharing means possession in common.[23] When we look at the Song and Ming Neo-Confucian writings on the Confucian classics, it can be seen that their success rested in their absorption of Buddhism, leading to a broad and profound philosophy.

Fourthly, the hermeneutics of classics essentially has the character of practical philosophy. In order to distinguish hermeneutics from the old classical one, which simply treated itself as a methodology for avoiding mistakes and making correct interpretations, Gadamer especially emphasized that hermeneutics, as a philosophy, was simply practical philosophy. As he saw it, a look at the history of hermeneutics showed that since ancient times, the two types of hermeneutics—theological and jurisprudential—"were not so much theoretical as corollary and ancillary to the practical activity of the judge or clergyman who had completed his theoretical training."[24] According to Gadam-

---

22 *Ibid.*, p. 64.

23 *Ibid.* Paul Ricoeur has another interpretation on Gadamer's Aneignung: "'Appropriation' is my translation of the German term *Aneignung*. *Aneignen* means 'to make one's own' what was initially 'alien.' According to the intention of the word, the aim of all hermeneutics is to struggle against cultural distance and historical alienation." Paul Ricoeur, *Hermeneutics and the Human Sciences: Essays on Language Action and Interpretation*, p. 147.

24 Hans-Georg Gadamer, *Truth and Method: The Basic Characteristics of Philosophical Hermeneutics*, vol. 1, p. 3.

er, both the judge's rulings and the clergyman's sermons are beyond the scope of the scientific inquiry that confines itself to the objective object of the text; they have absolutely nothing to do with the question of scientific methodology, nor are they undertaken to construct exact knowledge that meets the ideals of scientific methodology. On the contrary, they are all concerned with the human experience and ultimate human concerns in the world as a whole. In this regard, we must give full play to the practical wisdom of the Chinese studies of the Confucian classics. Of course, we also have to be aware that the view of practice in such studies only stresses obligations and responsibilities, and neglects human rights and freedom; therefore, we must adopt rounded view of practice. For oneself and for becoming human, our understanding must use *Bildung*; the "rising up to humanity through culture" (*Emporbildung zur Humanität*) of Johann Gottfried Herder, or Hegel's abandonment of particularity and assimilation of strangeness, that will allow us to rise to universality. Gadamer said, "No longer dependent on retelling, which mediates past knowledge with the present, understanding consciousness acquires—through its immediate access to literary tradition—a genuine opportunity to change and widen its horizon, and thus enrich its world by a whole new and deeper dimension. The appropriation of literary tradition even surpasses the experience connected with the adventure of traveling and being immersed in the world of a foreign language."[25]

Fifth, classical hermeneutics is a philosophy that develops through a critical dialogue with tradition. Interpretation is actually dialogue. Gadamer said, "I know just one instance in which the interpretation of speech is not an additional supplemental moment, and in which we go to the essence of the matters themselves: that is dialogue. In the dialogue we are really interpret-

---

25 *Ibid.*, pp. 393-394.

ing. Speaking then is interpreting itself. It is the function of the dialogue that in saying or stating something a challenging relation with the other evolves, a response is provoked, and the response provides the interpretation of the other's interpretation. In this way, we know (an old Platonic insight) that the real mode of givenness of speech starts with dialogue. It is no longer a system of symbols or a set of rules of grammar and syntax. The real act of work is appropriation in the common being of the speakers. I try in my own work to develop this point of view, on how language, not in the sense of *langue*, but in the sense of real exchange and work, manifests itself in the dialogue. In any form of dialogue, we are building up. We are building up a common language, so that at the end of the dialogue we will have some ground. Of course, not every dialogue is fruitful, but it should at least aim at being a dialogue."[26]

Sixth, classical hermeneutics maintains that the development of consistency between interpreter and text is an endless process, and all consistency between one person and another is based on this premise. Heidegger said that the work of art meets us as a kind of thrust (*Stoß*). The experience of the text may always contain an experience of boundaries, and each reading that seeks to understand is just a step on a never-ending road. Whoever embarks on this path knows that he can never "cope with" his text, and that he must accept this thrust. This point, for the interpreter, is that man has recognized his own limitations. Gadamer always associated hermeneutics with the finitude of man, and opposed the concept of infinite intellect. He illustrated this with Plato's dialectical principle, "These 'principles' of Plato were not meant to yield an ultimate determinacy. I think Plato was well aware of this position when he said that philosophy is something for human beings, not for gods. Gods

---

26 Hans-Georg Gadamer, "Hermeneutics Questions and Prospects," p. 63.

know, but we are in this ongoing process of approximation and overcoming error by dialectically moving towards truth."[27] This view of the finitude of human cognition made Gadamer reject the concept of "infinite intellect." In a letter to Leo Strauss, he said, "What I believe to have understood through Heidegger (and what I can testify to from my Protestant background) is, above all, that philosophy must learn to do without the idea of an infinite intellect (*die Philosophie lernen muss, ohne die Idee eines unendlichen Intellektes auszukommen*). I have attempted to draw up a corresponding hermeneutics."[28] A philosophy understood from the starting point of previous dialogues and the restlessness that may again cause a problem will definitely be different from the currently dominant philosophy that is explored from the perspective of methodology. The true philosophy of the future must be a philosophy of hermeneutics.

Seventh, classical hermeneutics takes into account both ontology and methodology. Some people believe that Western hermeneutics is only about ontology, not methodology, but Paul Ricoeur already has presented a long route/short route theory.[29] The short route here refers to an ontology of understanding, which dissociates itself from any methodological discussion and directly brings itself to the ontological level; specifying that understanding is the mode of being of *Dasein*. The long route, on the other hand, refers to a kind of epistemology of interpretation that considers the methodological problems of interpretation and asks how we can provide an instrument for the interpretation and clear understanding of texts. In Ricoeur's view, the short route, i.e., the ontology of understanding, brought about a revolution in understanding and made understanding

---

27 *Ibid.*, p. 64.

28 Leo Strauss, *Return to Classic Political Philosophy*, p. 415.

29 Paul Ricoeur, "Existence and Hermeneutics," p. 249.

the direction of planning for *Dasein*, so that the question of truth was no longer a question of method but an obvious question of being. However, this does not truly solve our hermeneutic problem, and may indeed conceal it. We need to ask: How do we undertake the interpretation of texts? How are we to understand the finitude and infinity of interpretation? What is the truth dimension of interpretation? And how can conflicts between various opposing interpretations be arbitrated? Therefore, we must take the long route of the epistemology of interpretation, that is, we must supplement the short route of the analysis of *Dasein* with the long route starting with linguistic analysis. In this way, we remain connected to those disciplines that use methodology to seek real explanations and oppose the method that separates the truth, i.e., the typical features of understanding, from the disciplinary operating methods derived from exegesis. In other words, we must consider both ontology and methodology. Here, our country's long history and experience of classical interpretation will have ample space to demonstrate its prowess.

Eighth, research and dialogue on conceptual history are an important approach to classical hermeneutics. In using traditional concepts (benevolence, principle, etc.), this can neither be a pure acceptance that simply demonstrates erudition and antiquity, nor can it be a technical operation that turns these concepts into tools. Rather, it should revive and develop these concepts on the basis of their historical origins. Gadamer discussed several major leading humanistic concepts, saying that "This kind of thinking must be aware of the fact that its own understanding and interpretation are not constructions based on principles, but the furthering of an event that goes far back."[30] Our classical hermeneutics is research on conceptual history,

---

30 Hans-Georg Gadamer, *Truth and Method: The Basic Characteristics of Philosophical Hermeneutics*, vol. 1, p. 7.

which entails developing and enriching the connotations of concepts on the basis of their original historical meanings. This research is unlike etymology, which, although it also explores the historical origin of words, is an abstraction constituted by linguistic science rather than a living language. As Gadamer said, "It seems to me that my own contribution is the discovery that no conceptual language, not even what Heidegger called the 'language of metaphysics,' represents an unbreakable constraint upon thought if only the thinker allows himself to trust language; that is, if he engages in dialogue with other thinkers and other ways of thinking."[31]

To sum up, to develop a universal hermeneutics of the classics, we must first have a world-level philosophical vision and knowledge and must start from the highest philosophical achievements of today; next, we must find theories and methods deserving of being studied from the long history and experience of Western classical hermeneutics, especially those developed from early modern times and contemporary philosophical hermeneutics; at the same time, we must set out from China's long history of rich practice of classical interpretation, especially from the fields created by Confucian classical learning: philology, evidential learning, annotation, and studies of ancient characters and documents. On this dual foundation, we should develop a universal classical hermeneutics that is different from and higher than Western hermeneutics, and display to the world the theory and methodology of Chinese classical interpretation. This is, of course, a long and complex process that requires everybody's joint efforts and long-term exploration; in particular, it requires that China's researchers on Chinese and Western philosophy should throw themselves into this great enterprise.

---

31 Hans-Georg Gadamer, *Truth and Method: Supplements and Indexes*, vol. 2, p. 332.

References

Dilthey, Wilhelm. "The Rise of Hermeneutics. " In *Understanding and Interpretation: Classics of Hermeneutics*, ed. Hong Handing. Beijing: The Oriental Press, 2001.

Dong, Zhongshu. *Chunqiu Fanlu*. Shanghai: Shanghai Chinese Classics Publishing House, 1986.

Eckermann, J .P. *Conversations with Goethe* . Trans . Zhu Guangqian . In *Collected Works of Zhu Guangqian*. Hefei: Anhui Education Press, 1989.

Feng, Tianyu. *The Spirit of Confucian Classics*. Shanghai: Shanghai People' Publishing House, 2014.

Gadamer, Hans-Georg. "The Hermeneutics of Suspicion." In *Hermeneutics Questions and Prospects*, eds. Gary Shapiro and Alan Sica. Amherst, MA: University of Massachusetts Press, 1984.

— — . *Gesammelte Werke 5*. Tübingen: J.C.B. Mohr (Paul Siebeck), 1993.

— — . *Gesammelte Werke 9*. Tübingen: J.C.B. Mohr (Paul Siebeck), 1993.

— — . *Truth and Method: Supplements and Indexes*, vol . 2. Trans . Hong Handing . Beijing: The Commercial Press, 2017.

— — . *Truth and Method: The Basic Characteristics of Philosophical Hermeneutics*, vol. 1. Trans. Hong Handing. Shanghai: Shanghai Translation Publishing House, 2004.

Jing, Haifeng. *The Modern Interpretation of Chinese Philosophy*. Beijing: People' Publishing House, 2018.

Ricoeur, Paul. "Existence and Hermeneutics." In *Understanding and Interpretation: Classics of Hermeneutics*, ed. Hong Handing. Beijing: The Oriental Press, 2001.

——. *Hermeneutics and the Human Sciences: Essays on Language Action and Interpretation*. Trans. and ed. John B. Thompson. Cambridge: Cambridge University Press, 1981.

Sima, Qian. *Records of the Grand Historian: Hereditary House of Confucius*. Beijing: Zhonghua Book Company, 1963.

Strauss, Leo. *Return to Classic Political Philosophy*. Trans. Zhu Yanbing and He Hongzao. Beijing: Huaxia Publishing House, 2006.

Yang, Naiqiao, ed. *China's Classical Confucian Hermeneutics and Western Hermeneutics*. Shanghai: Zhongxi Publishing House, 2016.

Zhou, Dunyi. *Zhou Zi Tong Shu*. Shanghai: Shanghai Chinese Classics Publishing House, 2000.

Zhou, Guangqing. *Introduction to Chinese Classical Hermeneutics*. Beijing: Zhonghua Book Company, 2002.

Zhu, Xi. *Jin Si Lu*, ed. Lu Zuqian. Shanghai: Shanghai Chinese Classics Publishing House, 2010.

——. *Si Shu Zhang Ju Jizhu*. Beijing: Zhonghua Book Company, 1983.

(Translated by Deyuan Huang)

Meine Begegnung mit Gadamer[1]

1.

Die schwierigen Jahre der Übersetzung von
Wahrheit und Methode

Auf Gadamers Buch *Wahrheit und Methode* stieß ich 1983, als ich mit einem Stipendium des bundesdeutschen Humboldt-Forschungsfonds Gastwissenschaftler an der Universität München war. Meine ursprüngliche philosophische Bildung in China richtete sich neben der traditionellen Philosophie vor allem auf die angloamerikanische analytische Philosophie, so dass ich, als ich in zeitgenössische deutsche philosophische Kreise eintrat, mit deren zeitgenössischer Philosophie sehr wenig vertraut war. Ich erinnere mich, dass ich einmal sehr überrascht war, das Wort Hermeneutik im Universitätslehrplan zu sehen, und ich fragte einen jungen Doktor an der Universität München nach diesem Begriff, und es geschah durch die Empfehlung dieses Doktors, dass ich auf Gadamers Buch aufmerksam wurde. Ich erinnere mich, dass dieser Doktor damals sagte, wenn ich die heutige Philosophie in Deutschland verstehen wolle, müsse ich zuerst dieses Buch lesen. Später habe ich in meiner Philosophie-Lehre an mehreren deutschen Universitäten festgestellt, dass, obwohl einige deutsche Philosophen Gadamers Ansichten nicht vollständig teilten, es immer ein tiefes hermeneutisches Bewusstsein in ihren Vorlesungen gab und sogar eine breite Verwendung einiger philosophisch-hermeneutischer Begriffe.

---

1 Dieser Artikel wurde zuerst veröffentlicht in: *Eksistenz. Philosophical Hermeneutics and Intercultural Philosophy*, Bd.1, Berlin 2022, S. 113-124.

Diese eigene Erfahrung machte mir klar, dass unsere Forschung zur westlichen Philosophie zu dieser Zeit mindestens zwanzig oder dreißig Jahre hinter dem Westen zurücklag. Ich erinnere mich, dass sich Gadamer in seinen späteren Jahren an die Schwierigkeiten bei der Veröffentlichung seines Buches *Wahrheit und Methode* erinnerte und sagte:

> Die Sache mit dem Titel des Buches war schwierig genug. Meine Fachgenossen im In- und Ausland erwarteten es als eine philosophische Hermeneutik. Aber als ich dies als Titel vorschlug, fragte der Verleger zurück: Was ist das? In der Tat war es besser, damals das noch fremde Wort in den Untertitel zu verbannen. [2]

War die Hermeneutik in Deutschland in den frühen 1960er Jahren noch ein Fremdwort für den gewöhnlichen Verleger, so war das Wort im China der frühen 1980er Jahre nicht nur für die gewöhnlichen Menschen, sondern auch für die professionellen Philosophen ein Fremdwort. Ich erinnere mich, dass ich Ende 1979 am Institut für Philosophie der Chinesischen Akademie der Sozialwissenschaften an einer Informationsveranstaltung für Delegierte teilnahm, die von einem Hegel-Seminar in Deutschland zurückkehrten, und bei der die Frage aufgeworfen wurde, was für eine Philosophie die Hermeneutik sei. Dies zeigte, dass es eine offensichtliche Distanz zwischen uns und den westlichen Gelehrten in der philosophischen Forschung gibt, und nur mit einem klaren Bewusstsein für diese Distanz können wir unsere philosophische Forschung verbessern.

1984 wechselte ich von der Universität München zum Philosophiestudium an die Universität Düsseldorf. Mein akademischer Berater war Professor Lutz Geldsetzer, ein junger

---

2 Hans-Georg Gadamer, *Wahrheit und Methode*, Bd. 2, Tübingen: Mohr Siebeck, 1993, S. 493.

Verschiedene Versionen der chinesischen Übersetzung
von Wahrheit und Methode

deutscher Philosoph, der mehr als zehn Sprachen fließend beherrschte und nicht nur mit Griechisch, Latein und Hebräisch vertraut war, sondern auch mit Chinesisch, Japanisch und Sanskrit. Sein breites Wissen über die Geschichte der Philosophie ermöglichte ihm, im Alter von etwa 40 Jahren die Position eines Universitätsprofessors für Philosophie zu erlangen. Das ist heute in Deutschland eine Seltenheit. Wir waren im gleichen Alter und hatten gemeinsame Interessen, und wir wurden bald akademische Vertraute. Wir haben in Deutschland an der Zusammenstellung von drei Bänden des Lexikons der chinesischen Philosophie mitgearbeitet,[3] und waren Mitautoren des Buches *Grundlagen der chinesischen Philosophie*.[4] Professor Geldsetzer hat durch die Herausgabe einer Reihe klassischer Lektüren zur Hermeneutik einen einzigartigen Beitrag zum Studium der deutschen Hermeneutik geleistet, eine Reihe, dank derer ihn Gadamer in *Wahrheit und Methode* dreimal erwähnt und in höchsten Tönen gelobt hat: „Über die ältere Geschichte der Hermeneutik kann man sich inzwischen auch noch auf andere Weise gut unterrichten, seit Lutz Geldsetzer eine Reihe von hermeneutischen Neudrucken ins Leben gerufen hat", und „Geldsetzer hat diesen Neuausgaben sehr sorgfältige, mit erstaunlicher Gelehrsamkeit erarbeitete Einleitungen beigegeben."[5] In dieser wissenschaftlichen Atmosphäre begann ich, *Wahrheit und Methode* zu studieren. Um ehrlich zu sein, war es jedoch ein sehr schwer zu lesendes Werk, und trotz der gelegentlichen Klärung meiner Zweifel durch Geldsetzer war es für mich, der keinen Hintergrund in diesem Thema hatte, immer noch nicht einfach, den Inhalt des Buches wirklich zu verstehen. Um des Verständ-

---

3 Lutz Geldsetzer und Handing Hong, *Chinesisch-deutsches Lexikon der chinesischen Philosophie*, Aalen: Scientia Verlag, 1986, 1991, 1995.

4 Lutz Geldsetzer und Handing Hong, *Grundlagen der chinesischen Philosophie*, Stuttgart: Reclam Verlag, 1998.

5 Gadamer, *Wahrheit und Methode*, Bd. 2, S. 463.

nisses willen besorgte ich mir damals auch eine englische Übersetzung, aber diese erste englische Übersetzung (1975) brachte mir stattdessen mehr Missverständnisse. Erst als mein guter Freund, Professor Wei-Xun Fu, mir eine zweite englische Übersetzung (1991) aus den Vereinigten Staaten schickte, war ich in der Lage, Gadamers *Wahrheit und Methode* richtig zu verstehen.

Nachdem ich 1985 nach China zurückgekehrt war, begann ich auf Drängen und Betreiben einiger Freunde mit der Übersetzung dieses Buches. Mein Grund für das Übersetzen war damals vor allem, es genauer zu lesen und zu verstehen. Ich habe nie um des Übersetzens willen übersetzt; meine Übersetzungsarbeit wurde von meinen Untersuchungen geleitet. Ich habe *Wahrheit und Methode* damals noch aus einem anderen Grund übersetzt, nämlich, wie ich im Nachwort der Übersetzung des Buches angegeben habe:

In gewisser Weise scheint es, dass ich mehr verloren als gewonnen habe, indem ich so lange an der Übersetzung nur eines Werkes gearbeitet habe. Einige meiner Freunde und Verwandten haben mir das auch vorgeworfen und gesagt, dass ich die gute Zeit der häufigen Auslandsreisen und des direkten Kontaktes und akademischen Austauschs mit deutschen Philosophen hätte nutzen können, um eine Monographie über Hermeneutik und sogar über zeitgenössische deutsche Philosophie zu schreiben. Obwohl an dieser Kritik etwas Wahres dran ist, vor allem angesichts der gegenwärtigen Tendenz der akademischen Bewertung in China, sich eher auf Abhandlungen als auf Übersetzungen zu konzentrieren, muss ich dennoch argumentieren, dass die Entwicklung der westlichen Philosophie bis zum heutigen Tag so umfangreich und tiefgreifend ist, dass sie nicht von einer einzigen akademischen Monographie abgedeckt werden kann, die in nur wenigen Jahren geschrieben wurde. Anstatt eine Monographie zu schreiben, die unsere eigenen unausgereiften Ansichten darlegt, sehe ich es als für unsere Leser wichtiger an, ein einflussreiches klassisches Werk zu übersetzen.

Es ist eine solche Überzeugung, die mich kein Bedauern über diese Jahre harter Arbeit empfinden lässt. Im Gegenteil, es ist eine Art Trost, in mein eigenes Herz zu schauen. Wenn unsere jungen Leser durch dieses Buch zu einem bodenständigen Studium der zeitgenössischen westlichen Philosophie geführt werden können, wird die jahrelange harte Arbeit des Übersetzers nicht umsonst gewesen sein. Ich denke, es scheint nicht überflüssig, aber umso notwendiger, diesen Punkt noch einmal zu betonen, besonders da unsere akademische Gemeinschaft heutzutage allgemein dazu neigt, in Eile zu sein.

Die Hermeneutik mag für einige unserer heutigen Leser nicht neu sein, aber auf jeden Fall ist sie erst seit etwa einem Jahrzehnt bekannt. In den späten 1970er Jahren wurden wir durch einige Übersetzungen der Philosophie aus Ostdeutschland und Japan mit diesem Begriff konfrontiert, waren aber völlig unwissend über seinen Inhalt. Erst in den 1980er Jahren, aufgrund des so genannten existenzialistischen Fiebers der Zeit, begannen einige einzelne Wissenschaftler, sich mit dieser zeitgenössischen westlichen philosophischen Tendenz zu beschäftigen, insbesondere 1986, als die vom Institut für Philosophie der Chinesischen Akademie der Sozialwissenschaften herausgegebene Zeitschrift *Philosophical Translation Series* einen Artikel mit dem Titel „Deutsche philosophische Hermeneutik" herausbrachte, der in gewissem Maße das Studium der Hermeneutik in China förderte. In dieser Zeit wurden in Chinas philosophischen Kreisen zwei Tagungen zur Hermeneutik organisiert. Eine davon war das erste Symposium zur Hermeneutik, das 1987 an der Universität Shenzhen stattfand und zu dem wir Professor Geldsetzer, einen deutschen Philosophiehistoriker, einluden, der einen Vortrag mit dem Titel „Was ist Hermeneutik" hielt. Die teilnehmenden chinesischen und ausländischen Philosophen diskutierten ausgiebig über die Geschichte der Hermeneutik, ihre wichtigsten Ansichten und den Unterschied zwischen Natur- und Geisteswissenschaften. Das zweite Symposium zur Hermeneutik fand 1991 in Chengdu statt, wo mehr als 30 Philosophen die Ideen von Heidegger, Gadamer, Habermas, Ricoeur und Derrida eingehend diskutierten. All diese Aktivitäten haben zweifellos das Studium der Hermeneutik in China gefördert, so dass die Hermeneutik heute ein spezielles Studiengebiet mit einer wachsenden Zahl von Forschern in China geworden ist. Es war in dieser Atmosphäre, dass meine Übersetzung von *Wahrheit und Methode* sich vollzog, fast zehn Jahre lang, beginnend 1986 und endend 1995.

Die deutsche Ausgabe von Gadamers *Wahrheit und Methode* ist bisher in fünf Auflagen erschienen, neben der Erstausgabe 1960 gab es überarbeitete Auflagen 1965, 1972, 1975 und eine Ausgabe 1986, die in Gadamers *Gesammelten Werken* aufgenommen wurde. Die 4. Auflage von 1975 war die Standardausgabe, ein einbändiges Werk von 553 Seiten, das neben dem Text von *Wahrheit und Methode* auch Anmerkungen, den Aufsatz „Hermeneutik und Historismus" und ein Nachwort zur 3. Auflage beinhaltet. Die 1986 erschienene Ausgabe (5. Auflage) wurde gegenüber der ursprünglichen 4. Auflage stark erweitert und zu einem zweibändigen Werk, wobei Band 1 (Hermeneutik I) den Hauptteil von *Wahrheit und Methode* darstellt und Band 2 (Hermeneutik II) insgesamt 31 Aufsätze zu *Wahrheit und Methode* vor und nach der Veröffentlichung versammelt, die in fünf Teile gegliedert sind: Einführung, Vorstufen, Ergänzungen, Weiterentwicklungen und Anhänge. Die beiden Bände umfassen insgesamt 1027 Seiten. Es gibt drei chinesische Ausgaben von Übersetzungen von *Wahrheit und Methode*, die ich übersetzt habe: eine Festlandausgabe mit zwei Volumen, die auf der Standardausgabe der 4. Auflage basiert und von der *Shanghai Translation Press* (1992, 1999) veröffentlicht wurde; eine Überseeausgabe des ersten und zweiten Bandes, die auf der 5. Auflage basiert und von der *Times Culture Publishing Company* in Taiwan (1993, 1995) veröffentlicht wurde; und eine überarbeitete Ausgabe der beiden Bände, die von der *Commercial Press* in Beijing (2007, 2011, 2013) veröffentlicht wurde.

Im Prozess der Übersetzung habe ich auf Joel C. Weinsheimers Buch *Gadamer's Hermeneutics: A Reading of Truth and Method* verwiesen, und für die etwas schwierigen Kapitel von *Wahrheit und Methode* habe ich sogar relevante Passagen aus Weinsheimers Buch übersetzt. Dies kann man als Grundlage meines Buches *Lektüre von Wahrheit und Methode* (《<真理与方法>解读》) bezeichnen. Natürlich ist Weinsheimers Paraphrase nicht ganz für chinesische Leser geeignet, und aus diesem Grund habe ich im spezifischen Prozess der Übersetzung von *Wahrheit und Methode* auch den Inhalt von Weinsheimers Paraphrase ein wenig nach meinem eigenen Verständnis erweitert. Dies war der Ursprung meiner *Lektüre von Wahrheit und Methode*. So können einige Teile der Paraphrase immer noch Weinsheimers Interpretation beibehalten, und sogar einige Passagen als Übersetzungen seines Buches bezeichnet werden. Dieses Buch mit dem Titel *Wahrheit des Verstehens* wurde 2001 von der *Shandong People Press* veröffentlicht.

Seit 2001 habe ich an mehreren Universitäten in Taiwan Seminare über *Wahrheit und Methode* gehalten, die von Master-Studenten und Doktoranden der Philosophie- und Chinesisch-Abteilungen besucht wurden. Ich habe das Format des Deutschen Seminars gewählt, bei dem die Studenten zusätzlich zu meinen Erklärungen im Voraus eine einführende Lektüre vorbereiten und am Ende eine Diskussion führen sollen. Im Laufe der Jahre zeigten mehrere Doktoranden großes Interesse an *Wahrheit und Methode*, und auf Anregung der jungen Doktoranden beschloss ich, das Buch *Wahrheit des Verstehens* zu erweitern, das vor mehr als zehn Jahren veröffentlicht wurde. Ursprünglich wollte ich mit Doktoranden wie Bo-Hong Lin, Bo-Lin Lai, Li-Ye Wang und Yu-Jia Xu daran arbeiten, und sie haben viel Zeit damit verbracht, es zusammenzustellen, aber da sie dann ihre Doktorarbeiten schreiben mussten und nicht viel Zeit dafür aufwenden konnten, und auch die Interpretation wirklich zu schreiben keine leichte Aufgabe für die Doktoranden war, also habe ich mich schließlich entschlossen, es alleine zu machen. Diese neue erweiterte Version von *Lektüre von Wahrheit und Methode* beinhaltet jedoch noch eine Menge, das aus der Mitarbeit mit Bo-Lin Lai und Bo-Hong Lin hervorgegangen ist.

Wie genau sollte ein exegetischer Text geschrieben werden? Die chinesische Tradition hat ein dreistufiges Muster der klassischen Exegese, bekannt als Kanon, Übertragung und Kommentar (经，传和注). In Übereinstimmung mit dieser Tradition versuche ich, diese dreistufige Struktur zu übernehmen. Erstens: Der Haupttext von Gadamers *Wahrheit und Methode* ist der Kanon, einige direkte Interpretationen des Haupttextes sind die Übertragungen, und weitere Ergänzungen zur ursprünglichen Interpretation sind die Kommentare. So ist unser Exemplar von *Lektüre von Wahrheit und Methode* in Groß- und Kleingedrucktes unterteilt, wobei das Großgedruckte die Übertragung und das Kleingedruckte der Kommentar ist. Da die Seitenzahlen von Ausgabe zu Ausgabe der chinesischen Übersetzung variieren (jede Ausgabe ist am Rand mit den deutschen Seitenzahlen der Ausgabe von 1986 versehen), werden in dieser *Lektüre* der Einheitlichkeit halber die deutschen Seitenzahlen vermerkt.

Abschließend muss ich darauf hinweisen, dass diese *Lektüre* nur eine Möglichkeit ist, das Buch *Wahrheit und Methode* zu lesen. Es bietet nur ein mögliches Verständnis von Gadamers Text, oder, man könnte sagen, ein mögliches Missverständnis, und deshalb dürfen wir es nicht als eine endgültige Interpretation betrachten. Sein Nutzen kann nur der eines Hinweises sein. Manchmal kann natürlich auch ein falscher Hinweis irgendwie erhellend sein.

2.

Meine beiden persönlichen Begegnungen mit Gadamer

Ich bin Gadamer zweimal begegnet, das erste Mal im Mai 1989, als ich zu einem internationalen Symposium in Bonn eingeladen war, um den hundertsten Geburtstag Heideggers zu begehen. Es war eine ziemlich große Tagung, die von der Alexander-Humboldt-Stiftung ausgerichtet wurde und an der einige der weltweit führenden Experten der Heidegger-Forschung teilnahmen. Gadamer hielt einen Vortrag zum Thema „Heidegger und die Griechen". Der Ton seines Deutsch war so ansprechend, fließend und intonierend, dass es für mich ein schöner Genuss war. Ich wurde sofort daran erinnert, wie ich dem amerikanischen Professor Wendt zuhörte, als er in den 1950er Jahren an der Abteilung für Fremdsprachen der Universität Peking englische Gedichte rezitierte. Ich nutzte die Pause in der Tagung, um Professor Gadamer zweimal aufzusuchen, der damals 90 Jahre alt, aber bei guter Gesundheit war. Einerseits erzählte ich ihm, dass ich *Wahrheit und Methode* ins Chinesische übersetze, andererseits bat ich ihn, mich über das Verständnis einiger Begriffe von *Wahrheit und Methode* aufzuklären. Zu meiner großen Überraschung war Gadamer selbst nicht an der Übersetzung des Buches interessiert und schlug sogar den Begriff „Unübersetzbarkeit" vor, als ob er Zweifel an der Übersetzbarkeit in die östlichen Sprachen hätte. Wenn wir vom An-

58

spruch der Vollkommenheit und der Korrektheit der Übersetzung ausgehen, müssen wir diese Unübersetzbarkeit zugeben,
denn vom hermeneutischen Standpunkt aus ist es unmöglich,
die Absicht und den Sinn des Autors eines Werkes, selbst für
den, der es schrieb, vollständig und objektiv auszudrücken. Das
Streben nach dem sogenannten einzig wahren objektiven Sinn
ist eine unerreichbare Illusion. Wenn wir jedoch – wie ich es
sehe – die Übersetzung auch als eine Art des Verstehens, der
Interpretation oder der Reproduktion betrachten – in der Tat ist
die früheste Interpretation des Wortes *Hermeneutik*, das neben
„Lehre von der Auslegung" auch „Lehre von der Übersetzung"
bedeutet –, dann dürfen wir die Übersetzung nicht herabsetzen,
weil sie die ursprüngliche Bedeutung des Originalbuches nicht
korrekt wiedergeben kann. In der Tat ist die Übersetzung eines
Buches, wie die Reproduktion aller Kunstwerke, eine Form der
Interpretation und damit die Art und Weise, wie dieses Buch
weiter existiert. Gadamer sagt in dritten Teil der *Wahrheit und
Methode* ausdrücklich:

> Jede Übersetzung ist daher schon Auslegung, ja man kann
> sagen, sie ist immer die Vollendung der Auslegung, die der
> Übersetzer dem ihm vorgegebenen Wort hat angedeihen
> lassen.[6]

Als meine Übersetzung der beiden Bände von *Wahrheit und Methode* 1995 von der *Times Culture Publishing Company* in Taiwan
veröffentlicht wurde, während ich Gastprofessor an der Universität Düsseldorf in Deutschland war, schickte ich das Buch an
Gadamer und sprach erneut über meine Ansichten zur Übersetzung. Gadamer, der damals 95 Jahre alt war, schrieb mir zurück
(13. November 1995) und sagte: „Jetzt müssen wir tatsächlich

---

6   Hans-Georg Gadamer, *Wahrheit und Methode*, Bd. 1, Tübingen: Mohr Sieb-
    eck, S. 388.

lernen, unseren Zentrismus über die eine oder andere Sprache zu überwinden. Sie haben zweifellos einen Einblick in die Geschichte der Hermeneutik bei Geldsetzer gewonnen, und deshalb unterstütze ich Ihre Bemühungen sehr." Es ist klar, dass Gadamer zu dieser Zeit auch weitere Ansichten über das Problem der Übersetzung in die östlichen Sprachen hatte.

Das zweite Mal traf ich Gadamer am 10. Juni 2001, als Professor Geldsetzer mich zu einem besonderen Besuch bei Gadamer nach Heidelberg begleitete. Gadamer war damals 101 Jahre alt, und in seinem Büro an der Heidelberger Universität unterhielten wir uns volle zwei Stunden lang. Was mich an diesem Gespräch am meisten berührte, war zum einen, dass Gadamer mir sagte, er sei voll von Sorgen, was die Zukunft der Welt angeht: „Die Chancen, dass sich die Rasse Mensch nicht selbst ausrottet, sind gering, wenn man bedenkt, dass so viel zerstörerische Kraft in den Händen des Menschen liegt." Das Ende der Welt, so stellte er mit Besorgnis fest, „ist von den Menschen selbst gemacht!" Wenn wir uns jetzt an den Schrecken der amerikanischen Twin Towers von 9/11 erinnern, der in jenem Jahr folgte, können wir nicht umhin, die Voraussicht dieses 101-jährigen Weltphilosophen zu bewundern. Zweitens sagte Gadamer, dass die Chinesen und Japaner früher nach Deutschland kamen, um Mathematik und Naturwissenschaft zu lernen, und deshalb Deutsch lernen mussten, aber heute scheine es keine solche Notwendigkeit zu geben. Möglicherweise habe die heutige Entwicklung der Wissenschaft im Fernen Osten dazu geführt, dass Westler das Bedürfnis verspürten, die chinesische Sprache zu lernen, und er betonte insbesondere, dass „in 200 Jahren wahrscheinlich jeder Chinesisch lernen wird, so wie heute jeder Englisch lernt". Drittens sagte Gadamer, dass „Hermeneutik eine Phantasie verlangt", dass wir in unserem Zeitalter der Wissenschaft und Technologie wirklich eine dichterische Vorstellungskraft brauchten, oder besser gesagt, eine dichterische Kultur. Es schien mir damals, dass er eine Vorahnung hatte, dass die dichterische Imagination oder die dichterische Kultur ein Balsam der Versöhnung im gegenwärtigen Zeitalter der Widersprüche und des Hasses sein könnte.

Kurz nach diesem Besuch schrieb Gadamer, im Alter von 101 Jahren, auch ein prägnantes Vorwort zur chinesischen Übersetzung von *Wahrheit und Methode*:

Es ist nun ein halbes Jahrhundert vergangen und ich empfinde eine große Genugtuung, daß ich bei der Gelegenheit Ihres Besuches in Heidelberg Ihre Bekanntschaft machen durfte, das ist mir noch sehr selten bisher begegnet, daß ein so großer Kenner der deutschen Philosophie, wie Sie sind, nun sogar meine eigenen Denkversuche für Ihre eigenen Landsleute aufgeschlossen hat.

Gewiß bekenne ich mich zu dem Vorrang des lebendigen Wortes, das die Menschen miteinander austauschen und verbinden.[7] Aber ein Land von dieser Ferne und dieser uralten Kultur macht es einen doch wirklich stolz, wenn nun meine eigenen Gedanken trotz meiner Ahnen Kant, Hegel, Nietzsche und Heidegger der lebendigen chinesischen Kultur zugänglich gemacht wird[8].

Man spürt geradezu die Lebensaufgabe, die wir alle für eine gemeinsame Zukunft der menschlichen Kultur zu leisten haben.

Zum Zeitpunkt meines Besuchs war Gadamer bei bester Gesundheit, und im Gegensatz zu meinen Lehrern, Herrn Lin He

---

7   Hier scheint ein grammatikalischer Fehler vorzuliegen. Was Gadamer vielleicht zu vermitteln versucht, ist: „das Wort, das die Menschen verbindet und möglich macht, sich miteinander auszutauschen".

8   Grammatikalischer Fehler. Hier sollte es „werden" heißen.

(贺麟)[9] und Herrn Youlan Feng (冯友兰)[10] hatte er gute Augen, Ohren und Hände und sah von außen nicht wie ein Hundertjähriger aus, aber er verstarb doch am 13. März 2002, weniger als zehn Monate nach unserem Besuch.

Für mich war es besonders traurig, weil Gadamer vor seinem Tod Forschungsmöglichkeiten und -mittel für mich an der Universität Heidelberg beantragt hatte. Als ich 2003 wieder in Deutschland war, bin ich natürlich nicht nach Heidelberg gegangen, weil es mir Kummer bereitet hätte, und ich war nur drei Monate an der Universität Düsseldorf.

(Übersetzt von Hongjian Wang und Karl Kraatz)

---

9   Lin He (20. September 1902 - 23. September 1992) war ein chinesischer Philosoph, Pädagoge und Übersetzer. Er war Vertreter des chinesischen Neokonfuzianismus und Spezialist für die Hegelschen Philosophie.

10 Youlan Feng (4. Dezember 1895 - 26. November 1990) war ein chinesischer Philosoph und Historiker der Philosophie. Er war als „moderner Neokonfuzianer" bekannt.

Bericht über Gadamers Vortrag
„Heidegger und die Griechen"

An einem hochkarätigen internationalen Heidegger-Symposium, das die Humboldt-Stiftung vom 25. bis 28. Mai 1989 in Bonn veranstaltete, nahmen einige der wichtigsten Philosophen auf dem Gebiet der zeitgenössischen deutschen Phänomenologie sowie einige bedeutende Heidegger-Schüler teil, darunter Gadamer, W. Biemel, F.-W. von Herrmann und K. Held. Als Humboldt-Stipendiat habe ich ebenfalls an der Konferenz teilgenommen. Nach der Eröffnungszeremonie am ersten Tag der Konferenz folgte Gadamers Hauptvortrag „Heidegger und die Griechen". Dies war wohl der wichtigste Vortrag des Heidegger-Symposiums. Der Saal war voll mit Zuhörern, von denen viele ohne Sitzplätze in den Gängen auf beiden Seiten des Saals standen. Ich sah, wie Professor Biemel aufgrund seines Beinleidens direkt vor dem Rednerpult auf dem Boden saß.

Anders als in früheren Vorträgen schien Gadamer uns ausländischen Philosophen gleich zu Beginn mitteilen zu wollen, dass sein Vortrag für uns vorbereitet worden sei: „Das Thema ‚Heidegger und die Griechen' hat mich seit langem und immer wieder beschäftigt. Wenn ich es vor einem Kreise von Fachgenossen, die ihre Studien zu einem guten Teile in anderen Ländern betrieben haben und als Gäste dann auch mit uns in Deutschland und an den deutschen Universitäten lebten, wähle, gewinnt das Thema einen ganz besonderen Akzent."[1] Gadamer führte uns ausländische Forscher in die Tiefen des Heideg-

---

1   Hans-Georg Gadamer, *Gesammelte Werke*, Bd. 10, Tübingen: Mohr Siebeck, 1995, S. 31.

gerschen Themas ein, in die Tiefen unserer Auseinandersetzung mit den zeitgenössischen deutschen Philosophen über das wichtige Heideggersche Thema. Wenn man, so Gadamer, trotz aller aktuellen Einwände gegen Heideggers politische Verstrickung in die katastrophalen Ereignisse des Dritten Reiches und trotz der Opposition anderer philosophischer Schulen wie der analytischen Philosophie fragen würde, wer der größte Philosoph des zwanzigsten Jahrhunderts war und wer am prominentesten in der philosophischen Literatur vertreten ist, dann wäre es, abgesehen von Wittgenstein, wohl Heidegger. Was genau ist die *Bedeutung* Heideggers? Gadamer fragt: „Es drängt sich unmittelbar als besonderer Gesichtspunkt auf: Was ist es eigentlich an Heidegger, was ihn zu einem so bevorzugten Studiengegenstand in der großen philosophischen Weltöffentlichkeit erhoben hat [...]?"[2]

Bevor Gadamer jedoch die Frage nach der Bedeutung Heideggers weiter beantworten konnte, machte er uns ausländische Forscher auf den wichtigen Punkt aufmerksam, dass wir uns nicht auf die Übersetzung verlassen sollten, um Heidegger zu verstehen, indem er sagte:

> Bei allem Eifer und aller Einsicht in die Notwendigkeit von Übersetzungen dürften wir uns doch wohl unter uns im klaren sein, daß man nicht auf dem Wege von Übersetzungen in einen wirklichen philosophischen Austausch eintreten kann. Es ist bekanntlich mindestens seit Plato umstritten, ob man Philosophie überhaupt auf schriftlichem Wege übermitteln kann, und jedenfalls ist es unbestritten, daß man auf der Basis von Übersetzungen zu keinem echten Austausch zu gelangen vermag, wenn es sich um philosophische Gespräche handeln soll.[3]

---

2   Gadamer, *Gesammelte Werke*, Bd. 10, S. 31.

3   Ebd.

Gadamer wies darauf hin, dass das Verstehen eines Denkers einen direkten Dialog mit ihm erfordere und dass wir deshalb einen Philosophen nicht allein durch eine Übersetzung verstehen könnten. Diese Ansicht wurde später durch einen Vortrag mit dem Titel „Unübersetzbarkeit" von einem anderen Philosophen, Prof. von Herrmann, auf der Konferenz untermauert. Gadamers Vortrag über „Heidegger und die Griechen" beinhaltete zwei für uns bedeutsame Themen: Das eine behandelte Heidegger und die griechische Philosophie, dessen Kern die Beziehung zwischen griechischer und deutscher Philosophie war, das andere, wie ausländische Gelehrte aus verschiedenen Kulturkreisen Heidegger und die deutsche Philosophie verstehen könnten. Der Kern dieses Themas war die Frage, wie eine Sprache eine andere, fremde Sprache versteht und ob die Übersetzung den Sinn einer anderen, fremden Sprache einholen kann.

Wie aus dem vollständigen Bericht hervorgeht, äußerte sich Gadamer jedoch nur wenig zum ersten Thema, obwohl er die Notwendigkeit eines stärkeren kulturellen Austausches zwischen Forschern aus verschiedenen Kulturkreisen betonte. Das steht ganz im Gegensatz zu seinem Aufsatz „Die griechische Philosophie und das moderne Denken" von 1978, wo Gadamer einleitend sagt: „Man hat geradezu von der Gräkomanie des deutschen Philosophierens gesprochen, und das Wort ist sicherlich nicht nur für Heidegger oder die Marburger Schule des Neukantianismus gültig. Es ist ebenso für die große Bewegung des deutschen Idealismus selber gültig, der — von Kant inspiriert — von Fichte bis Hegel eine unmittelbare Rückwendung zu den Denkanstößen der platonischen und aristotelischen Dialektik unternommen hat."[4] Gadamer sagte einerseits, dass wir nie vergessen dürften, dass die griechische Philosophie keine

---

4 Hans-Georg Gadamer, *Gesammelte Werke*, Bd. 6, Tübingen: Mohr Siebeck, 1985, S. 3.

Erste Begegnung mit Gadamer in Bonn am 26. Mai 1989

Philosophie in dem engen Sinne ist, den wir heute mit diesem Wort verbinden, sondern dass sie eine Philosophie mit einer universellen Bedeutung ist, und andererseits, dass es zweifellos die Griechen waren, die mit ihren besonderen Ideen eine weltgeschichtliche Entscheidung einleiteten und den Weg der modernen Zivilisation durch die Schaffung der Wissenschaft bestimmten.[5]

Gadamer spricht hier nicht über Heideggers Verhältnis zur griechischen Philosophie, sondern darüber, wie Heidegger die griechische Philosophie verstanden hat. Wie ist dies gemeint? Ich denke, dass es hier einen sehr wichtigen Hinweis gibt. Denn wenn Heidegger vorschlägt, dass wir uns bei dem philosophischen Verstehen nicht auf die Übersetzung verlassen können, stellt dies eine Herausforderung für die Hermeneutik dar. Wir wissen, dass das wesentliche Merkmal der Hermeneutik das Verstehen antiker oder fremder Texte durch Übersetzung und Interpretation ist. Wenn Gadamer davon spricht, dass wir trotz allen Eifers und trotz aller Einsicht in der Übersetzung niemals ein echtes philosophisches Verstehen auf dem Boden der Übersetzung erreichen könnten, ist dann die Hermeneutik überhaupt noch relevant? Hier scheint Gadamer an das wahre Verstehen direkt im verbalen und lebendigen Dialog zu appellieren und zu argumentieren, dass wir nur durch die direkte Rede und den Dialog den Sinn eines philosophischen Textes einholen könnten. Wie wir wissen, war Gadamer in seinen späteren Jahren so begeistert von der lebendigen Sprache, dass er einmal sagte, er

---

5 „Was das Abendland, was Europa, die so genannte ‚westliche Welt', von den großen hieratischen Kulturen der asiatischen Länder unterscheidet, ist ja gerade dieser neue Aufbruch des Wissenwollens, der mit der griechischen Philosophie, mit der griechischen Mathematik, mit der griechischen Medizin, mit dem Ganzen ihrer theoretischen Neugier und ihrer intellektuellen Meisterschaft verbunden ist. So ist für das moderne Denken die Konfrontation mit dem griechischen Denken eine Art Selbstbegegnung." Gadamer, *Gesammelte Werke*, Bd. 6, S. 3.

habe eine Abhandlung mit dem Titel „Sprache und Sprechen“ geschrieben, in der es um die Idee gehe, dass das Zuhören dem Sprechen übergeordnet sei und dass das Zuhören von Sprache wie das Genießen oder Wertschätzen der „Sprachmelodie“ eines Gespräches sei.

Diesem Rückgriff Gadamers auf den lebendigen Dialog hatte der zeitgenössische französische Philosoph Paul Ricoeur entgegengehalten: „Der Dialog ist der Austausch von Fragen und Antworten; es gibt keinen solchen Austausch zwischen dem Autor und dem Leser; der Autor antwortet dem Leser nicht. Das Schreiben trennt den Akt des Schreibens und den Akt des Lesens in zwei Aspekte, und es gibt wenig Kommunikation zwischen den beiden. Der Leser ist weit entfernt vom Akt des Schreibens und der Autor vom Akt des Lesens.“[6] Nach Ricoeur ist der Hauptgegenstand der Hermeneutik der Text, der festgelegte Diskurs, und wenn der Diskurs zum Text wird, findet hier eine Bedeutungsumwandlung statt, nicht in dem Sinn, auf den sich der ursprüngliche Diskurs bezieht, sondern in dem Sinn, den der Leser im Lichte seines eigenen Kontexts und seiner realen Probleme versteht. Stellt Gadamer die Hermeneutik vor ein Problem, wenn er hier auf die mündliche und lebendige Rede zurückgreift und argumentiert, dass die Übersetzung allein noch kein philosophisches Verstehen bedeuten kann?

Das Bedürfnis, das Verhältnis zwischen Textinterpretation und lebendiger Rede zu erhellen, ist daher wohl das Hauptanliegen von Gadamers Bericht. Er will seine Aussagen über die lebendige Rede und den Dialog mit der Hermeneutik verbinden. Wahre Texthermeneutik sollte nach Gadamer dialogische Hermeneutik sein, d.h. das Verstehen von Texten wird als Dialog mit ihnen begriffen, mit dem philosophischen Verstehen als einer besonderen

---

6 Paul Ricoeur, *Hermeneutics and the Human Sciences. Essays on Language, Action and Interpretation*, edited and translated by John B. Thompson, Cambridge: Cambridge University Press, 1981, S. 147.

Art des gegenseitigen Verstehens, um so antike und fremde Texte durch die existentielle Hermeneutik in der Gegenwart lebendig werden zu lassen. In dieser Form des Dialogs besteht die Beziehung zwischen dem Interpreten und dem Text. Es handelt sich nicht um eine Beziehung zwischen „Ich" und „Es", sondern um eine Beziehung zwischen „Ich" und „Du". Das Verstehen des Textes ist also das Verstehen der Verbindung zwischen „Ich" und „Du", das gegenseitige Verstehen des Textes im Dialog zwischen zwei Menschen. In dieser dialogischen Beziehung ist der Text als Gegenstand, der verstanden oder interpretiert werden soll, nicht etwas Feststehendes und Abgeschlossenes, sondern eindeutig etwas, das lebendig und für uns relevant ist.

Wenn Gadamer sagt, dass wir uns nicht auf Übersetzungen verlassen sollten, um die Werke fremder Philosophen zu begreifen, müssen wir zunächst betonen, dass er meint, dass wir uns nicht auf Übersetzungen allein verlassen dürften, und nicht, dass wir keine Fremdsprachen lernen sollten. Tatsächlich misst Gadamer dem Verstehen fremder Texte durch das Studium von Fremdsprachen große Bedeutung bei, wie wir in Gadamers Aufsatz „Über das Hören" lesen können:

> Wenn wir uns in der Welt von morgen zurechtfinden sollen, wird es für die junge Generation der Zukunft von entscheidender Wichtigkeit sein, daß das enge Zusammenleben zwischen den verschiedenen Kulturen und Sprachwelten ein gegenseitiges Sich-verstehen möglich werden läßt. Das bedeutet aber, daß man möglichst fremde Sprachen lernen muss, und vor allem, so weit lernen muss, daß man nicht mehr übersetzt oder gar Übersetztes liest, sondern daß man selber in der Sprache des Anderen denkt und die Sprache des Anderen versteht. Das mag utopisch klingen, aber die Erfahrung lehrt, daß die Lebenssituation wie die Luft, die man atmet, unhörbar von der Sprache wiedertönt.[7]

---

7   Hans-Georg Gadamer, *Hermeneutische Entwürfe. Vorträge und Aufsätze*, Tü-

Denken und Verstehen in einer Fremdsprache bedeutet hier ein lebendiges Verstehen von fremden Texten. Voraussetzung für dieses lebendige Verstehen ist, dass ich den Text oder die andere Person als ein „Du" und nicht als ein „Es" sehe. So schreibt Gadamer weiter: „Wenn Menschen zusammenkommen und sich fremd fühlen, als Fremde, die in einem Land agieren, dann ist es eine realistische Aufgabe für die Zukunft, sich mit den Werten des anderen zu identifizieren, auch wenn es Unterschiede in der kulturellen Welt gibt. Wenn wir von Europa zu einer geeinten Welt kommen wollen, dann müssen wir das lernen."[8]

Damit kehren wir zum Thema dieses Berichts zurück, nämlich Heidegger und die Griechen. Tatsächlich versucht Gadamer in diesem Bericht nicht, über die Beziehung zwischen Heidegger und der griechischen Philosophie oder zwischen der deutschen Philosophie und der griechischen Philosophie zu sprechen, sondern darüber, wie Heidegger die griechische Philosophie verstanden hat. Mit dieser Frage will er das Verhältnis von lebendigem Diskurs bzw. Dialog und Textinterpretation thematisieren, denn Heideggers Verständnis der griechischen Philosophie, d.h. Heideggers Verständnis der griechischen philosophischen Texte, ist ein inhärent hermeneutisches Problem, aber dieses hermeneutische Problem wird für Heidegger wiederum durch den lebendigen Dialog, d.h. durch das Verständnis des Sinns der lebendigen Möglichkeiten der griechischen Texte, bewältigt. Im Folgenden wird analysiert, was Gadamer in diesem Bericht konkret zu dieser Problemstellung gesagt hat.

Gadamer beginnt diesen Bericht mit der Feststellung, dass in der Frage, wie Heidegger die griechische Philosophie verstanden hat, nun ein neuer Durchbruch gelungen sei, nämlich die Entdeckung zweier früher Heideggerscher Texte, nämlich

---

bingen: Mohr Siebeck, 2000, S. 52.

8   Gadamer, *Hermeneutische Entwürfe*, S. 52.

„Phänomenologische Interpretationen zu Aristoteles. Anzeige der hermeneutischen Situation" (1922) und „Ontologie: Hermeneutik der Faktizität" (1923). Gadamer ist zunächst der Meinung, dass die beiden jüngeren Heideggerschen Vorlesungen im Vergleich zum Stil der späteren nicht die gleiche „Gewalt" hätten. Was ist also wirklich revolutionär an diesen frühen Texten? Zunächst sei das, so Gadamer, die Sprache. Diese beiden Texte erlaubten es uns, tiefer zu verstehen, wie Heidegger die griechische Philosophie durch die lebendige Sprache verstanden habe. Nach Gadamer führen diese beiden Texte einen wichtigen Begriff ein, nämlich Faktizität. Heideggers Manuskript sei von Anfang an durch den Klang des Wortes „Faktizität" bestimmt gewesen. Gadamer sagt dazu:

> Das Wort „Faktizität" ist selber schon ein wichtiges Zeugnis. Es ist ein Wort, das offenkundig ein Gegenwort sein will, ein Wort gegen alles das, was im deutschen Idealismus etwa als Bewußtsein, Selbstbewußtsein, Geist oder auch als das transzendentale Ego Husserls im Schwange war. Man spürt in diesem Ausdruck „Faktizität" sofort den neuen Einfluß Kierkegaards, der seit dem Ersten Weltkrieg das zeitgenössische Denken erschütterte, und indirekt auch den Einfluß Wilhelm Diltheys mit seiner ständigen Mahnfrage des Historismus, die er an den Apriorismus der neukantianischen Transzendentalphilosophie richtete.[9]

Auf dieser Grundlage entwickelt Heidegger die Konzeption der Hermeneutik der Faktizität. Betrachtet man die griechische Philosophie aus einer solchen Hermeneutik heraus, so zeigt sich die Geschichtlichkeit des Menschen in der „Jeweiligkeit", und diese Jeweiligkeit des Menschen steht immer vor der Aufgabe, sich in ihrer Faktizität zu artikulieren.[10]

---

9 Gadamer, *Gesammelte Werke*, Bd. 10, S. 34.

10 So sagt Gadamer: „Jedenfalls hat er [Heidegger], wenn er auch bei den Griechen den Anfang unserer Geschichte suchte, dies nicht als ein Hu-

Heidegger bezeichnete das Wesen philosophischer Aussagen bekanntlich als „formale Anzeige". Damit wollte er sagen, man könne im Denken höchstens in die Richtung des zu Verstehenden zeigen. Man müsse die eigenen Augen benutzen und die Anstrengung auf sich nehmen, selber hinzuschauen. Dann erst werde man die Sprache finden, mit der das gesagt werden könne, was man „sieht".[11] So ist Heideggers Begriff der „formalen Anzeige" zu verstehen. Sie erfordert eine Orientierung am Konkreten und ist gleichsam eine Aufforderung zur Konkretisierung. Betont wird der praktische Vollzugssinn, wodurch sich der Bezug zum Gegenstand, über den ausgesagt wird, verändert. Der Bezug sei nun nicht mehr vorherbestimmt, beispielsweise durch die Tendenz des Verfallens, der von Heidegger große Bedeutung zugedacht werde, sondern er sei radikal frei. Der formal anzeigende Begriff gibt den Gegenstand eben nicht vollständig und in einem eigentlichen Sinne, sondern ist von Heidegger nur als ein Hinweis vorgesehen, ein echter Hinweis, der prinzipiell vorgibt, wie der Gegenstand „gehabt", d.h. verschieden verstanden werden kann. Die formale Anzeige sei ein Hinweis, dass das Verstehen von Begriffen eine Verstehensaufgabe für jeden Einzelnen darstelle.

Jede Sprache ist eine Selbstdarstellung des menschlichen Lebens. Heidegger hat dies schon sehr früh bei der Konzeption seiner Hermeneutik der Faktizität berücksichtigt. Gadamer legt besonderen Wert auf diese Funktion der Heideggerschen Hermeneutik der Faktizität: das Konzept unseres sprachlichen Diskurses mit Leben zu erfüllen. Diese Funktion sei nicht abstrakt, sondern spreche aus der Erfahrung der Menschen und mache

---

manist getan, nicht als ein Philologe oder Historiker, der seiner Tradition fraglos folgt. Er gehorchte vielmehr seinem kritischen Bedürfnis angesichts seiner eigenen Daseinsnot." Gadamer, *Gesammelte Werke*, Bd. 10, S. 39.

11 Vgl. Gadamer, *Gesammelte Werke*, Bd. 10, S. 42.

uns durch gelebte Erfahrung deutlich, was ein Begriff aussagen wolle. So könnten wir zum Beispiel von Heidegger lernen, dass das griechische Wort für „Sein" oder „Ousia", wie es von Platon und Aristoteles verwendet wird, in Wirklichkeit das Eigentum von Bauern bedeute: seine Anwesenheit, all jene Dinge, die für den Bauern in seiner Arbeit verwendet und für Hausarbeiten gebraucht werden könnte. Gadamer betont, dass es nicht Heideggers Entdeckung sei, dass „Ousia" diese ursprüngliche Bedeutung hat. Sie finde sich schon bei Aristoteles, zum Beispiel in den begrifflichen Kategorien von Buch V der *Metaphysik*. Aber was für Aristoteles noch selbstverständlich gewesen sei, werde von Heidegger zum ersten Mal erläutert, nämlich dass sich unsere Begriffe aus dem Gebrauch der Worte unserer Sprache heraus entwickelten. Auf diese Weise werde die Entstehung der menschlichen gelebten Erfahrung nachvollziehbar. Aus Heideggers Ausführungen könnten wir lernen, dass Ousia Anwesenheit bedeute und deshalb einen Zeitsinn einschließe. Gadamer führt weiter aus:

In Wahrheit ist es in anderen Sprachen, und vor allem in den Sprachen, die nicht dem europäischen Kulturkreis angehören, erst recht so, daß der natürliche Sprachgebrauch im Aussagenbereich von Dichtung und Meditation immer mitspricht. Wir haben hier in einer interessanten Diskussion etwa die Tatsache behandelt, daß im Chinesischen „Tao" eigentlich „Weg" heißt. Da sind wir auf einmal nicht durch einen Kontinent und durch Jahrhunderte oder Jahrtausende vom heutigen China entfernt, wenn die Griechen dafür „Methodos" sagten – was den Weg meint, den man nachzugehen hat. Dies griechische Wort ist freilich bei den Griechen nicht der neuzeitliche Begriff der Wissenschaftstheorie. Heidegger sagte lieber „Wege" statt „Werke".[12]

---

12 Gadamer, *Gesammelte Werke*, Bd. 10, S. 41.

Gadamer erklärt dieses Verhältnis des Verstehens anhand des Verhältnisses von Wort und Begriff. In einem Artikel über die Bedeutung der griechischen Philosophie sagte Gadamer: „Ich beziehe mich auf das Verhältnis von Wort und Begriff bei den Griechen. Es handelt sich um einen unvergleichlichen Aktualitätston, der allen, die die griechischen Texte gelesen haben, entgegenklingt."[13] Das griechische Wort sei ursprünglich alt, aber in unserem hermeneutischen Verständnis sei es zu einem Wort mit Aktualitätston geworden. Gadamer zitiert den griechischen Begriff der Psyche, den Descartes bekanntlich mit dem Begriff res cogitans übersetzt hat, aber Descartes' res cogitans ist ein reines Selbstbewusstsein, und dieses Selbstbewusstseins, als das fundamentum inconcussum aller Erkenntnisgewissheit, wird zur gemeinsamen Voraussetzung einer neuen Philosophie. Diese neue Philosophie sei mächtig genug gewesen, um alle bisherigen Denkrichtungen zu überwinden, seien sie empiristisch oder idealistisch, positivistisch oder materialistisch. Gadamer argumentiert jedoch, dass die Bedeutung des griechischen Wortes „Seele" aus der Sicht der späteren deutschen Philosophie über dieses moderne Verständnis der Seele hinausgehe und sich tatsächlich auf das Prinzip des Lebens beziehe und die Seele somit auch die Bedeutung von „Wachstumsgeist" oder vegetativum einschließe. Denn, so Gadamer, wenn eine organische Lebensform erwacht, „wächst" sie nicht an einem anderen Organismus wie ein Kristall an einem anderen Kristall oder eine Schneeflocke, die zu einem Schneeball geknetet wird. Vielmehr bedeutet Wachstum die weitere Ausdehnung des Ganzen selbst. Es ist also nach Gadamer eine Assoziation mit sich selbst inmitten eines Ortes, an dem schon immer etwas gewachsen ist. Das zeige, dass das, was in der Philosophie über die Seele gesagt wurde, richtig sei: nämlich, dass sie hier

---

13 Gadamer, *Hermeneutische Entwürfe*, S. 99.

die Reflexion, die Zurückbezogenheit sei. Aber die Reflexion sei nicht auf das Selbstbewusstsein beschränkt; sie sei in der Tat nie zuerst im Selbstbewusstsein. Das Selbstbewusstsein sei kein Anknüpfungspunkt, der dem organischen Wesen durch eine eingeschränkte Selbstassoziation eingeschrieben sei, sondern im Gegenteil, die Selbstreflexion sei als Darstellung der höchsten Ebene der biologischen Selbstassoziation eingeschrieben, die auf der „Einheit" des Geschöpfes beruhe. So sagt Gadamer:

> Hegel drückt das Subjekt auf eine neue Weise aus: nämlich mit seiner Theorie des objektiven Geistes. Die Bildung eines solchen Begriffs ist wie ein Rückgriff auf die Griechen. Wenn etwas am Denken der Neuzeit einzigartig ist, dann bedeutet dies, dass es als individuelle Subjekte gedacht werden kann, die sich allein auf der Grundlage der Subjektivität einigen. Und Hegel lehrt nun mit seiner Lehre vom objektiven Geist, dass es Formen des Geistes gibt, die wir als Geist erkennen und die im Bewusstsein des Subjekts nicht richtig gedacht und bewusst werden. Dabei handelt es sich wahrscheinlich um wichtige Institutionen wie die Familie und die Gesellschaft, den Staat, das Recht und die Sprache. Hegels Wendung vom „objektiven Geist", die de facto dem ganzen Staatsdenken der späteren eineinhalb hundert Jahre zugrunde liegt, ist im Grunde eine Übersetzung aus dem Griechischen. Es ist zwar überhaupt kein griechisches Wort darin, sondern die Wendung enthält außer dem lateinischen Begriff des Objektiven den deutschen, aus der Mystik mit Inhalt aufgeladenen, ursprünglich stoischen und dann neutestamentlichen Begriff von Geist (pneuma).[14]

Auf den ersten Blick, so Gadamer, gibt sich Heidegger nicht so viel Mühe wie die Linguisten, denn ihm geht es nicht um die

---

14 Gadamer, *Hermeneutische Entwürfe*, S. 103.

Akzeptanz eines Wortes oder die Einhaltung von Regeln, sondern um die Ausbildung eines ständigen Horizonts und einer Offenheit für das Andere, zu der jeder sprachfähig ist. Wenn wir aber genauer hinschauten, dann sähen wir, dass Heidegger aus diesem Mangel heraus eine wahrhaft bahnbrechende Anstrengung aufbringe, das Denkvermögen und die Vorstellungskraft der Sprache miteinander zu verschmelzen.

Für Gadamer war Heidegger in dieser Hinsicht der Größte, d.h. er verstand es, auf die geheimen Ursprünge der Wörter und ihre geschichtliche Verbergung aufmerksam zu machen. Heidegger wusste, „die Vielstelligkeit von Worten und die innere Gravitationskraft lebendigen Wortgebrauchs und seiner Begriffsimplikationen freizulegen und unseren Sinn dafür zu schärfen [...], das scheint mir jedoch das bleibende Erbe, das er uns hinterließ und das uns hier alle eint. Das war der positive Sinn von ‚Destruktion', in dem nichts von Zerstörung mitklang."[15] Gadamers Schlusswort lautete:

> Auf seine Weise hat auch das Denken stets nach dem Wort zu suchen, das uns so ausspricht, und gewiß wird ein jeder im Ausgang von seiner eigenen Muttersprache immer wieder die Öffnung zur Welt durchmessen müssen, aus der ihm das rechte Wort für ihn kommt, in dem ihm das Gemeinte aufgeht – in welchen Sprachen der Begriffe es immer ist. Denken ist in Wort und Begriff wie das Dichten in Wort und Bild. Da wird nichts wie ein bloßes Werkzeug gebraucht. Da wird etwas in die Helle gehoben, in der „es weltet" – um mit einem Wort Heideggers zu schließen.[16]

(Übersetzt von Wei Chen und Karl Kraatz)

---

15 Gadamer, *Gesammelte Werke*, Bd. 10, S. 45.

16 Gadamer, *Gesammelte Werke*, Bd. 10, S. 45.

Blick nach Osten vom Philosophen des Jahrhunderts

Aufzeichnung des Besuchs bei Gadamer.

Vorwort des Autors

Am 11. Juni 2001 besuchte ich Professor Hans-Georg Gadamer, der damals 101 Jahre alt war, in seinem Büro an der Universität Heidelberg in Deutschland, begleitet von Professor Lutz Geldsetzer von der Universität Düsseldorf. Dieser Besuch war wahrscheinlich der letzte akademische Besuch im Leben Gadamers, bei dem er ausländische Gelehrte empfing. In diesem Interview äußerte Gadamer nicht nur seine tiefe Besorgnis über die Zukunft der Menschheit und seine Überzeugung, dass es kaum eine Chance gebe, dass die Rasse Mensch sich nicht selbst zerstöre, sondern er sprach auch über die Zivilisationen im Osten und im Westen und über sein sicheres Gefühl, dass der Westen den Osten für intellektuelle Anregungen nutzen sollte. Er sagte, dass es wahrscheinlich sei, dass in zweihundert Jahren jeder Chinesisch lernen werde, so wie heute jeder Englisch lernt.

Kurz nach dem Besuch schrieben Geldsetzer und ich jeweils eine Zusammenfassung des Gesprächs in unserer Landessprache. Mein Beitrag mit dem Titel "Blick nach Osten vom Philosophen des Jahrhunderts. Aufzeichnung des Besuchs bei Gadamer" wurde am 25. Juli desselben Jahres in einer chinesischen Zeitung (China Reading Weekly) veröffentlicht. Die deutsche Fassung dieses Artikels finden Sie hier.

Yizhai, Peking, 30. April 2021

Seit zwei ganzen Monaten bin ich in Deutschland, und heute kann ich sagen, dass es der Höhepunkt meines kurzen Besuchs in Deutschland war: ein Treffen mit Professor Hans-Georg Gadamer, dem berühmtesten deutschen Philosophen der Gegenwart und Begründer der philosophischen Hermeneutik, der jetzt einhundertundeins Jahre alt ist. Herr Geldsetzer vom Philosophischen Seminar der Universität Düsseldorf hatte Professor Gadamer im vergangenen Monat telefonisch mitgeteilt, dass ich den weiten Weg aus Peking gekommen sei, um ihn zu besuchen, dass ich der chinesische Übersetzer seines Meisterwerks *Wahrheit und Methode* sei und dass ich mich seit fast zwanzig Jahren auf seine philosophische Hermeneutik spezialisiert hätte. Gadamer war so erfreut, dass er am Telefon sagte, er könne am 11. Juni zwei Stunden lang mit uns sprechen. Ah! Ein hundertjähriger Mann konnte noch ein zweistündiges Gespräch führen - und ich nahm es mit Vorsicht.

Um pünktlich zu sein, fuhren Professor Geldsetzer und ich am Morgen des 10. Juni um elf Uhr los. Die Entfernung von Düsseldorf nach Heidelberg betrug fast vierhundert Kilometer. Wir fuhren durch Koblenz, die landschaftlich schönste Region in Mitteldeutschland. Dem Vergnügen zuliebe verließen wir die Autobahn und fuhren den Weg entlang dem Rhein. Mittags aßen wir in dem bekannten Touristenort Boppard. Gegen 17:00 Uhr kamen wir in Heidelberg an. Nachdem wir uns in unserem Hotel eingerichtet hatten, spazierten wir durch Heidelberg. Ich war vor 18 Jahren in Heidelberg gewesen, und der Eindruck, den es auf mich hinterlassen hatte, war eine alte Fußgängerzone, ein altes Schloss, eine alte Brücke, eine alte Universität, ein Philosophenweg und immer Regenwetter. Heute schien das alles sich zu wiederholen. Wir besuchten die Schloss-Ruine bei leichtem Nieselregen. Das Schloss wurde im 1689 von

Besuch bei Gadamer am 11. Juni 2001

französischen Truppen Ludwigs XIV und nochmals 1693 von frz. Pionieren zerstört und es sind nur noch wenige, aber gewaltige Reste erhalten. Später soll auch Schiller für die Zerstörung dieses Gebäudes, das für ihn den feudalen Despotismus repräsentierte, eingetreten sein und gesagt haben, die Revolutionäre müssten es ganz zerstören. Das Verhältnis zwischen Deutschland und Frankreich war so heikel, dass die Franzosen heute noch von Nietzsche als gelegentlich deutschsprachigem französischem Revolutionär sprechen. Als ich vor 18 Jahren das erste Mal hier war, war das Schloss eine düstere Trümmerruine, aber diesmal war es so restauriert worden, dass es stellenweise wie neu gebaut wirkte.

Der nächste Morgen war wieder verregnet, und damit das Treffen reibungslos vor sich gehen konnte, fuhren wir sehr früh zur Universität Heidelberg, um das Gelände zu erkunden. Auf der rechten Seite der alten Fußgängerzone liegt die Universität Heidelberg, eine gut erhaltene alte Universität, berühmt zur Zeit Spinozas, der vom deutschen König eingeladen wurde, als Professor nach Heidelberg zu kommen, und nur deshalb ablehnte, weil er Bedenken hatte, ob er dort in voller Freiheit lehren könne. Laut Professor Geldsetzer war dieses Misstrauen von Spinoza berechtigt, denn die Studenten galten damals bei den deutschen Herrschern als gefährlich, und deshalb wurden die Universitäten damals vorsichtshalber nicht in großen Städten, sondern in kleinen Orten wie Heidelberg, Erlangen etc. angesiedelt. Ich hatte gedacht, dass das philosophische Seminar der Universität Heidelberg eine uralte Quelle der Philosophie sei, nicht nur in der Vergangenheit mit großen Philosophen wie Hegel, sondern auch mit weltbekannten Professoren wie Gadamer, die heute dort sitzen, und dass es ziemlich viele Professoren und viele Vorlesungen geben müsse, aber als ich mir den Stundenplan mit nur drei Vorlesungen ansah, musste ich mit einem gewissen Gefühl sagen, dass das goldene Zeitalter der Philosophie in Heidelberg vorbei sein könnte. Wir gingen vom zweiten Stock hinunter in den ersten Stock und fanden schließlich Gadamers Büro in einer Seitenecke. Obwohl Gadamer 1968 in den Ruhestand getreten war, reservierte die Universität dieses Büro weiterhin für ihn. Neben seinem Büro befand sich das Büro von Professor Rüdiger Bubner, dem heutigen Protagonisten der Heidelberger Philosophie.

Am Nachmittag klarte der Himmel auf und die Sonne kam zum Vorschein. Gegen vier Uhr kamen wir nach Verabredung an der Tür von Gadamers Büro im philosophischen Seminar der Universität Heidelberg an, und nachdem wir geklingelt hatten, öffnete seine Sekretärin die Tür. Das war ein Raum von etwa zwanzig Quadratmetern, und sobald wir eintraten, sah ich einen alten Mann, der etwas an seinem Schreibtisch schrieb. Und als wir das Zimmer betraten, schaute er auf, begrüßte uns mit einem Lächeln und bat uns, einen Moment zu warten, bis er das Schreiben beenden und sofort mit uns sprechen würde. Das gesamte Büro war mit Büchern in den Regalen und auf dem Boden rundherum gefüllt, bis auf seinen Schreibtisch und eine Reihe von Sofas in der Mitte. Das Sofa war alt und hatte offensichtlich mehr als nur ein paar Dutzend Jahre bei seinem Besitzer verbracht. In zwei Minuten, nachdem die Sekretärin Gadamer die von ihm unterschriebenen Papiere abgenommen hatte und aus dem Zimmer gegangen war, erhob sich Gadamer langsam von seinem Schreibtisch und ging mit leichtem Zittern auf Krücken zum Sofa; ich versuchte, ihn zu stützen, aber er sagte, nein, er könne sich selbst hinsetzen. Ich stellte mich Gadamer zunächst vor und teilte ihm mit, dass wir uns vor zehn Jahren bei einer Heidegger-Tagung in Bonn kennengelernt hätten, was er vergessen zu haben schien, und als ich meine kürzlich erschienene Interpretation von Gadamers *Wahrheit und Methode* herausholte und auf ein darin abgedrucktes Foto hinwies, das ich damals mit ihm gemacht hatte, lächelte er und sagte: „Ja, ja, ich erinnere mich, wir saßen am Abendtisch, um eine Mahlzeit zu essen." Ich fragte ihn zuerst gemäß der chinesischen Tradition nach seinem Zustand und sagte, dass wir chinesischen Intellektuellen gerne das Geheimnis seiner Langlebigkeit kennen würden. Er sagte, dass er jeden Tag um 11 Uhr ins Bett gehe, um 7 Uhr morgens aufstehe und jeden Montagnachmittag um 16 Uhr in seinem Büro sein müsse, um mehr als zwei Stunden zu arbeiten. Das einzige Geheimnis seiner Langlebigkeit sei, dass er seit 50 Jahren keinen Arzt besucht habe, obwohl er seit Jahrzehnten auf Krücken gehe. Seine Gesundheit führte er auf seinen Vater zurück, der Chemiker war. Er sagt, sein Vater habe ihm als Kind durch Experimente die Wirkung von Medikamenten und die Gefahren von Nebenwirkungen beigebracht, so dass er seitdem keine chemischen Medikamente mehr genommen habe und nie in einem Krankenhaus gewesen sei. Ich erinnerte mich daran, dass er, als ich ihn vor zehn Jahren in Bonn traf, damals einen guten Appetit hatte und nicht nur viel Sprudel trank, sondern auch viel Fleisch aß, und dass ich, obwohl ich mehr als vierzig Jahre jünger war als er, einen viel schlechteren Appetit hatte als er. Und als ich sagte, dass dies vielleicht der Schlüssel zu seiner Langlebigkeit sei, lachte er sofort und sagte, dass er noch viel trinke.

Da ich Chinese bin, sprach er, als er sich an seinen Vater erinnerte, über die früheren freundschaftlichen Beziehungen seines Vaters zu den Chinesen und den Japanern. Zu jener Zeit gab es einige chinesische und japanische Gelehrte im Universitätslabor seines Vaters und sein Vater pflegte sie als Gäste in sein Haus einzuladen, besonders am Neujahrstag. Diese Asiaten schenkten seiner Familie zum Neujahrsfest immer etwas chinesischen Satin, der damals in Europa sehr teuer war, und Gadamer sagte schmunzelnd: „Während und nach dem Ersten Weltkrieg trug unsere Familie Satinkleidung, obwohl es für Deutsche damals schwierig war, sich zu kleiden."

Zunächst erzählte Gadamer, dass er ununterbrochen gelesen und geschrieben habe, und er sagte, dass er in letzter Zeit an einer Arbeit mit dem Titel „Sprache und Sprechen" arbeite, in der es um den Vorrang gehe, der dem Sprechen und dem Zuhören zukomme, und darum, der Sprache zuzuhören, so als ob man die „Sprachmelodie" eines Gesprächs genieße oder schätze. Ich kenne das gut von Gadamers Hauptvortrag „Über die Griechen" auf der Bonner Tagung, wo seine Sprache ein musikalischer Genuss war. Gadamer sagte, dass die Schönheit der Sprache im Klang liege, und wenn wir den Klang einer Sprache mit Verständnis hören könnten, dann sei sie sehr schön. „Ich weiß zwar nicht, ob unsere deutsche Sprache im Vergleich zu Ihrer chinesischen Sprache schön ist, aber ich denke, die deutsche Sprache ist sehr musikalisch, und die Musikalität der Sprache kommt in unseren Gedichten zum Ausdruck." Er sagte, dass er manchmal einige Wörter vergesse, dass er aber in der Lage sei, diese Vergesslichkeit durch euphemistische Ausdrücke zu kaschieren, so dass es niemand merke. Wir sagten, dass das Vergessen zum Leben dazugehöre, dass viel Müdigkeit zurückbleibe und dass man sich so auf das Wesentliche konzentrieren könne, und das wurde von ihm voll bestätigt. Angesichts von Gadamers Betonung des Klangs und des Hörens schlug Professor Geldsetzer vor, ich solle ein chinesisches Gedicht in chinesischer Sprache vorlesen, und als ich eines von Li Taibai vorlas, nämlich „das Geräusch der Affenhufe auf beiden Seiten des Flusses ist unerschöpflich, und das leichte Boot hat zehntausend Berge überquert (两岸猿声蹄不尽，轻舟已过万重山)", hörte Gadamer aufmerksam zu und sagte, langsam nickend: „Leider kann ich es nicht verstehen. Freilich müsste ich oft bei Ihnen sein, um mich an diesen Ton zu gewöhnen." Aber als Professor Geldsetzer den figurativen Charakter der chinesischen Schrift vorstellte, betonte Gadamer, dass die Chinesen und Japaner früher nach Deutschland gekommen seien, um Mathematik und Naturwissenschaften zu studieren, und deshalb Deutsch hätten lernen müssen, aber heute erscheine es unnötig, weil, wie er meinte, die Entwicklung der Wissenschaft im Fernen Osten es heute möglich gemacht habe, dass die Westler das Bedürfnis verspürten, die chinesische Sprache zu lernen, und er sagte, dass *es wahrscheinlich sei, dass in 200 Jahren alle Chinesisch lernen würden, genauso wie wir heute alle Englisch lernen.* Die Grundlage für diese Vorahnung mag in der bildhaften Natur der chinesischen Sprache liegen. So wie heute an den Orten, an denen die Welt am intensivsten interagiert, wie z. B. im Verkehrswesen und an touristischen Zielen, oft figurative Zeichen verwendet werden, damit Reisende, die die Sprache nicht sprechen, sie schnell verstehen können, so hat die chinesische figurative Sprache, unabhängig vom Klang, einige Vorzüge gegenüber der westlichen artikulierten Sprache und könnte in Zukunft leichter zu verstehen sein. Außerdem ist die Bevölkerung Chinas heute mehr als eine Milliarde Menschen und nimmt so viel Platz im Internet ein, dass, wenn man kein Chinesisch kann, fast die Hälfte dessen, was online ist, für Westler wie ein ungeöffnetes Buch ist. Als Gadamer die chinesischen Schriftzeichen in dem Buch, das wir ihm geschenkt haben, nämlich *Die Grundlagen der chinesischen Philosophie,* veröffentlicht im Reclam Verlag, betrachtete, sagte er sofort, dass sie nicht „geschrieben", sondern „gezeichnet" seien, wie es bei westlichen Briefen der Fall ist, die durch die Handschrift des Autors gekennzeichnet sind. Das, was „hermeneutisch" aus dem Charakter der Handschrift des Autors abzuleiten sei, sei mehr als bloße Meinung über ihn.

Als wir ihn fragten, ob er von der Autorität und dem Ruf seines angesehenen Vaters beeinflusst worden sei, verneinte er dies rundheraus. Er sagte, dass sein Vater ursprünglich wollte, dass er Naturwissenschaften studiere, aber er habe stattdessen Literatur und Philologie gewählt. Sein Vater habe sich ihm jedoch nicht sofort widersetzt, sondern ihm im Gegenteil seine reiche Büchersammlung anbeboten, durch die er seine Wünsche noch einmal überdenken konnte. Er erinnerte sich, dass er damals trotz der Warnungen seines Vaters zwei Bücher von Nietzsche auswählte, weil er die Sprache dieses Buches als so schön empfand. Nur hatte sein Vater Nietzsche nie als Philosoph gesehen.

Unser Gespräch drehte sich natürlich um die Philosophie. Gadamer betonte zunächst den großen Einfluss seines Marburger Lehrers Paul Natorp, dem er einen Großteil seines Denkens verdanke. Von Heidegger sagte er, er habe ihn einige Jahre später getroffen. Er lachte und sagte, dass dieser Mann nicht sehr viel von ihm gehalten habe. Gadamer erinnerte sich daran, dass Heidegger anfangs dachte, sein Griechisch sei nicht gut, und dass er dann so hart daran gearbeitet habe, Griechisch zu lernen, dass Heidegger schließlich bemerkte, dass er in ihrem gemeinsamen Studium der alten Sprachen, insbesondere des Griechischen, besser war als Heidegger, und ihn deshalb in dieser Hinsicht als Gesprächspartner akzeptierte. Gadamer sagte weiter, dass Heideggers Betrachtungsweise sehr anschaulich gewesen sei, aber sein Verhältnis zur Poesie sei nicht gut. Gadamer betonte: *„Heidegger ist sehr gut im Denken, so bin ich ihm in dieser Hinsicht vielleicht unterlegen. Jedoch ist Heidegger zu sehr auf Begriffe fokussiert, während er für den musikalischen Aspekt von Dichtung oder Sprache keinen Sinn hat, und in dieser Hinsicht übertreffe ich ihn vielleicht.“*

Mit der Musikalität der Sprache kamen wir zu Nietzsche, der bekanntlich einen tiefen Sinn für die Musikalität der deutschen

Sprache hatte. Aber Gadamer schien, im Gegensatz zu Heidegger, keine hohe Meinung von Nietzsche zu haben; er hält ihn nicht für einen wahren Philosophen. Wenn Professor Geldsetzer davon sprach, dass Nietzsche heute von den Franzosen besonders beachtet werde und ein französischer Schriftsteller sogar gesagt habe, Nietzsche sei eigentlich ein französischer Denker, der sich beiläufig des Deutschen bedient habe, flüsterte uns Gadamer zu: *„Wussten Sie, dass Heidegger einmal gesagt hat, Nietzsche habe ihn kaputt gemacht?"* Das mag daran liegen, dass der späte Heidegger sein eigenes unehrenhaftes Verhalten verteidigte. Zu Heideggers Verhältnis zu den Nazionalsoziealisten sagte Gadamer, dass niemand, nicht einmal er selbst, die „Torheit" von Heideggers Verstrickung mit dem Nationalsozialismus in jener Zeit verstehen konnte. Gadamer sagte, dass er selbst immer auf die praktische Weisheit der Politik geachtet habe. Wir fragten uns, ob Heidegger eine „imperialistische" Haltung in der Philosophie gehabt habe, und Gadamer sagte nach kurzem Nachdenken: „Das mag sein." Dazu, ob dies auf Heideggers Eitelkeit zurückzuführen sei, sich als der Denker an der Spitze zu sehen, der die intellektuellen Bewegungen seiner Zeit lenke und sie vielleicht zu einer Richtungsänderung veranlasse - ein Anspruch, den Heidegger aufgab, sobald er merkte, dass er dies nicht kann -, würde uns interessieren, was Gadamer davon hält. Aber Gadamer wollte Heidegger nicht widersprechen. Er erklärte einfach, dass Heideggers Haltung aus seinem „Bauerntum" stammte. Gadamer betonte aber auch, dass diese Heideggersche Bauernschläue ihn später nicht daran gehindert habe, seine philosophische Gabe des Denkens und Zeigens zu entwickeln. Außerdem war Gadamer darüber beruhigt, dass Heidegger nach dem Zweiten Weltkrieg umdenken konnte. Er sagte, dass Heidegger später sehr besorgt gewesen sei, dass „die Leute ihn wegen seiner Verwicklung in den Nationalsozialismus nicht für einen würdigen Mann halten würden, und ich habe ihm in dieser Hinsicht geholfen, so sehr, dass er mir am Ende dankbar war".

Auf diese Weise erklärte uns Gadamer Heidegger, der von früh an von religiösen Fragen gequält worden sei. In dieser Hinsicht habe er sich der Prägung durch seine katholische Erziehung nie entziehen können. Obwohl er sich in Marburg mit Bultmann – einem bekannten protestantischen Theologen und Entmythologisierer – auseinandergesetzt habe (Professor Geldsetzer sagte, es sei ein religiöser Sektenstreit gewesen), sei er damit nicht erfolgreich gewesen. So könnten wir Heideggers spätere Hinwendung zur Poesie als aus dieser religiösen Aura kommend verstehen. Heideggers Lieblingsdichter sei Hölderlin gewesen, und dieser Dichter erahnte eine göttliche Dimension. Bei der Erwähnung von Hölderlin sagte Gadamer: „Goethe und Schiller, allen bekannt, und Hölderlin war damals unbekannt, aber heute, dank Heideggers Empfehlung, ist Hölderlin eine Berühmtheit." Heideggers Interpretationen der Dichtung hält Gadamer für unrichtig, sie fielen nämlich zu weit hinter Heideggers Arbeit am phänomenologischen Denken zurück. Das liege vor allem an Heideggers mangelndem Gespür für die Melodie der deutschen Sprache, eine Sprachmelodie, die für Gadamer von Interesse sei. Gadamer erzählte auch, dass er Heidegger kurz vor seinem Tod gesehen habe, als dieser sehr krank war und blass und schwach erschien. Gadamer sagte: *Ich war früher immer nicht in der Lage, eine Art echten Dialog mit Heidegger zu führen, weil er diese Eigenschaft hatte, dass er nicht wollte, dass sein Gesprächspartner seine Ansichten im Voraus errät, so dass er seinen Gesprächspartner zwingen musste, die Entwicklung seines Denkens nach und nach zu verfolgen. Aber ich bin immer besorgt, dass ich außerhalb seiner Spurweite laufe, und er will ein solches Gespräch nicht führen. Wir schienen also immer in einer kontradiktorischen Be-*

ziehung zu stehen, obwohl wir großen Respekt voreinander hatten." Bei diesem letzten Besuch aber wollte Heidegger einen Dialog mit ihm führen, und so kann man sagen, dass dies ein echter Dialog war, nur leider war es der letzte, und er war kurz.

Hinsichtlich der Sprachkenntnisse teilte Gadamer mit, dass er alle Sprachen Westeuropas, die sich aus dem Lateinischen entwickelt haben, fließend beherrsche und lese. Natürlich beherrschte er auch altes Griechisch. Allerdings bedauerte er, dass er die vom Griechischen abgeleiteten osteuropäischen Sprachen nie studiert habe und ihm daher die slawische Welt verschlossen geblieben sei. Er hatte eine russische Übersetzung von *Wahrheit und Methode* neben seiner Couch liegen - leider könne er kein Russisch, sagte er. Zur Rolle der Sprache wiederholte Gadamer noch einmal, dass *das Leben der Sprache im Sprechen liege,* und er sagte, er habe in der Vergangenheit die tiefe Erfahrung gemacht, dass die Darstellung der Wahrheit nicht in Lehrbüchern liege, sondern im lebendigen Gespräch mit Schülern. Er pflegte mit seinen Studenten nach den Seminaren in Cafés oder Weinlokale zu gehen, wenn sie, wie er sagte, frei von allen Formen waren und sich frei unterhielten, wovon sie alle sehr profitierten. Und einige Studenten sagten sogar, dass die besten Erkenntnisse nach dem Seminar gewonnen worden seien.

An dieser Stelle stellte ich die Frage: „Wie sehen Sie die Zukunft der Hermeneutik?" Gadamer sagte mit klarer Stimme: *„Es ist wahr, dass die Hermeneutik eine Phantasie oder Einbildung braucht."* In unserem Zeitalter der Wissenschaft und Technologie, sagte er, brauchen wir eine poetische Vorstellungskraft, ein Gedicht oder eine poetische Kultur. Er sprach von einem langen Weg zurück, wenn er in allgemeiner Form aufzeigte, dass die moderne Welt und ihre mathematischen Naturwissenschaften und Technologien ihren Ursprung letztlich der griechischen Kultur und der hermeneutischen Anwendung ihrer Philosophie und Wissenschaft verdankten. Er sagte: *„Die Chinesen können heute in der Welt nicht ohne Mathematik, Physik und Chemie existieren, Wissenschaften, die ihren Ursprung in Griechenland haben. Aber die Kraft dieser Wurzel ist heute verdorrt, und die Wissenschaft wird sich in Zukunft von anderen Wurzeln ernähren, vor allem aus dem Fernen Osten.“* Unbewusst wiederholte er seine Vorhersage, dass *die Menschen in zweihundert Jahren tatsächlich die chinesische Sprache lernen müssten, um alles gemeinsam zu begreifen oder zu genießen.* Andererseits müsse die Hermeneutik auch etwas Primitiveres erforschen, etwa das „Ägyptische“, das Griechenland so tiefgreifend beeinflusst habe, dass Platon im *Timaios* den Besuch eines Griechen in Ägypten so ernsthaft (und gründlich) beschreibt: „Was wissen wir davon, und wie können wir mehr darüber erfahren?“ Und wie hängt das mit dem Arabischen zusammen? Die arabische Kultur und ihre Ideen wurden von der griechischen Kultur überformt und wirkten lange Zeit als Katalysator für die westliche Kultur.

Gadamer drückte, wenn auch nicht explizit, deutlich seine Unzufriedenheit mit der regionalen Enge des sprachlich-hermeneutischen Horizonts Europas und des Westens aus und plädierte dafür, dass wir uns die Sprache und das Wissen anderer Kulturen aneignen sollten. Er bedauerte: „Leider ist es für mich zu spät!“ Aber er hoffte, dass die neue Generation hermeneutisch offen sei und bereit, sich das Beste aus fremden Kulturen anzueignen und es aufzunehmen.

Gadamer machte sich Sorgen um die Zukunft: *„Die Chancen, dass sich die Rasse Mensch nicht selbst vernichtet, sind sehr gering, wenn man bedenkt, welch große Zerstörungskraft in den Händen des Menschen liegt, obwohl es noch zu früh ist, um abschließend über die Zukunft zu urteilen.“* Er stellte mit Sorge fest: *„Das Ende der Welt kommt durch den Menschen selbst!“* Wenn es nicht die Atomkraft oder der künftige Atomkrieg, den die Menschen tatsächlich noch kontrollieren könnten, sei, dann sei es das chemische Gift, dank dem nicht nur die Menschheit, sondern alles Leben auf diesem Planeten ausgelöscht werden könne.

Schließlich sprachen wir über die chinesische Übersetzung von Gadamers Gesamtwerk. Er war natürlich hoch erfreut, dass sein Werk ins Chinesische übertragen wurde, aber er bedauerte, als er erfuhr, dass die Übersetzungen der Gesamtwerke von Kant und Hegel in China noch nicht angefertigt worden waren. Er sagte, er wage nicht anzunehmen, dass es möglich sei, das Gesamtwerk eines zeitgenössischen deutschen Philosophen zu veröffentlichen, bevor die chinesischen Übersetzungen der Gesamtwerke von Kant und Hegel erschienen seien. Er versprach jedoch, sofort ein Vorwort für die chinesische Übersetzung seines Werkes zu schreiben. Schließlich überreichte er mir, dem Übersetzer von *Wahrheit und Methode*, freundlicherweise eine neue Ausgabe seines Gesamtwerkes und ein neu erschienenes Buch: *Hermeneutik, Ästhetik, praktische Philosophie - Hans-Georg Gadamer im Gespräch*, die er jeweils mit folgenden Inschriften versah: „Einen Besuch aus alter Ferne mit alter Bekanntschaft" und „Einen seltenen Besuch, in herzlicher Verbundenheit". Als ich vortrug, dass ich mir eine Forschungsmöglichkeit an seiner Seite in Heidelberg wünsche, sagte er sofort zu und hoffte, dass ich so bald wie möglich kommen würde.

Die Zeit war bereits ein Viertel nach sechs. Bei der Verabschiedung zitierte Professor Geldsetzer aus den Analekten des Konfuzius: „Ein Freund kommt von weit her, und so ist es glücklich (有朋自远方来，不亦说乎)", und Professor Gadamer sagte: „Ja! Das ist genau das Richtige." Als ich sagte, dass ich gerne möchte, dass er nach China komme, lachte der alte Mann herzhaft und sagte humorvoll: „Wollen Sie mir etwas antun?" Aber er lehnte nicht ab, er würde es in Betracht ziehen, wenn die chinesische Regierung ihm ein spezielles Flugzeug zur Verfügung stellen würde. Als ich mich verabschiedete und ihm die Hand schüttelte, sagte er sofort: „Wir sehen uns bald wieder!"

Düsseldorf , Ende Juni, 2001
(Übersetzt von Hongjian Wang)

Gadamer in China

Gadamers erste Erscheinung in China geht auf das Jahr 1963 zurück, als Oskar Beckers Rezension von Gadamers *Wahrheit und Methode*[1] ins Chinesische übersetzt und in der Zeitschrift *International Philosophy Today* veröffentlicht wurde. Erst in den 1980er Jahren rückte er erneut in den Fokus der Wissenschaft; eine Zeit, die als „Zweite Aufklärung" bezeichnet wird und in der eine große Anzahl von Artikeln und Übersetzungen zur Hermeneutik in der chinesischen akademischen Welt veröffentlicht wurde. Besonders erwähnenswert ist, dass die *International Philosophy Today* 1986 ein Sonderheft zur Hermeneutik herausgegeben hat, das auf große Resonanz gestoßen ist. In den 1990er Jahren wurde Gadamers Meisterwerk *Wahrheit und Methode* von Professor Handing Hong ins Chinesische übersetzt, was zu einer weiten Verbreitung von Gadamer und seinen hermeneutischen Gedanken in der chinesischen Wissenschaftswelt führte. Seitdem ist Gadamers Einfluss in China nicht nur in der Philosophie spürbar geblieben, sondern hat sich auch auf Literatur, Geschichte, Kunst, Rechtswissenschaft, Soziologie und Politikwissenschaft ausgeweitet.

Im Jahr 2002 wurde unter der Leitung von Handing Hong und Yong-Jun Fu die Zeitschrift *Chinesische Hermeneutik* gegründet und ein nationales Fachkomitee für Hermeneutik ins Leben gerufen. Seitdem ist die Verbreitung von Gadamers Den-

---

1 Oskar Becker, „Die Fragwürdigkeit der Transzendierung der ästhetischen Dimension der Kunst", *Philosophische Rundschau* 10 (1962), S.225-238.

ken in China kontinuierlich gewachsen. Bis 2019 wurden insgesamt sieben Hermeneutik-Forschungszentren an verschiedenen chinesischen Universitäten eingerichtet und insgesamt 18 Ausgaben der *Chinesischen Hermeneutik* veröffentlicht, was diese Zeitschrift zu einer wichtigen Plattform für das Studium von Gadamers Denken gemacht hat. 2016 wurde unter der Leitung von Handing Hong die chinesische Übersetzung der *Gesammelten Werke* Gadamers begonnen, und mit der Beteiligung und den gemeinsamen Bemühungen von Dutzenden von Hermeneutik-Forschern in China ist das Projekt nun weitgehend abgeschlossen.

Insgesamt nimmt das hermeneutische Denken Gadamers in der zeitgenössischen chinesischen Wissenschaftswelt eine einzigartige und wichtige Stellung ein. Aufgrund des interdisziplinären Charakters der Hermeneutik geht ihr Einfluss längst auch über die Philosophie hinaus. Aus Platzgründen wird hier jedoch nur die Gadamer-Forschung in der chinesischen *philosophischen* Gemeinschaft vorgestellt, die hinsichtlich der folgenden zwei Aspekte beschrieben werden kann: erstens, die Konzentration auf die praktisch-philosophischen Implikationen von Gadamers Hermeneutik; und zweitens, der Versuch, eine chinesische Hermeneutik der Klassiker zu entwickeln, die Gadamers philosophische Hermeneutik als Modell verwendet.

Die Dissertation von Ting-Kuo Chang, die in den 1990er Jahren in Heidelberg unter der Betreuung von Rüdiger Bubner entstanden ist, war wahrscheinlich die erste umfassende und systematische Untersuchung der Philosophie Gadamers durch chinesische Wissenschaftler.[2] Sie fand jedoch in China keine nennenswerte Resonanz, weil sie auf Deutsch verfasst wur-

---

2 Ting-Kuo Chang, *Geschichte, Verstehen und Praxis. Eine Untersuchung zur philosophischen Hermeneutik Hans-Georg Gadamers unter besonderer Berücksichtigung ihrer Annäherung an die Tradition der praktischen Philosophie*, Marburg: Tectum Verlag, 1994.

de. Bezeichnenderweise lag der Schwerpunkt dieser Dissertation gerade auf der praktischen Philosophie Gadamers. Als sich die Beschäftigung mit Gadamers Denken im chinesischen Sprachraum allmählich intensivierte, entdeckte die akademische Gemeinschaft die praktisch-philosophische Ausrichtung Gadamers. In diesem Zusammenhang wird häufig Gadamers in den 1970er Jahren aufgestellte Behauptung zitiert, dass „Hermeneutik Philosophie [ist], und als Philosophie praktische Philosophie".[3] Es muss hervorgehoben werden, dass sich chinesische Wissenschaftler unter dem Einfluss des marxistischen Denkens und des traditionellen chinesischen philosophischen Denkens besonders mit der praktischen Philosophie bzw. der praktischen Natur der Philosophie befassen.Die praktisch-philosophische Ausrichtung von Gadamers Hermeneutik passt zweifellos in dieses Muster und sie hat daher breite Aufmerksamkeit erhalten.

Da Heidegger in der chinesischen Wissenschaft seit jeher große Aufmerksamkeit genießt, gehört auch die Untersuchung der Beziehung zwischen Gadamer und Heidegger zu den aktuellen Themen. Durch die eingehende Untersuchung der Quelle von Gadamers Denken, d.h. des frühen Heideggers, wurde die innere Verbindung zwischen hermeneutischem Denken und aristotelischer praktischer Philosophie entdeckt. Im Vordergrund steht dabei die Modernisierung von Aristoteles' Konzept der φρόνησις [praktische Vernünftigkeit]. Es wurde zudem festgestellt, dass Gadamer im Gegensatz zu Heideggers durchgehend ontologischem Ansatz mit seiner Konzentration auf Ethos und Dialog eine hermeneutische Ethik entwickelt hat, die auf öffentlicher Vernünftigkeit beruht. Wegen der Betonung der Geschichtlichkeit in der hermeneutischen Tradition wurde Ga-

---

3 Hans-Georg Gadamer, „Hermeneutik als Praktische Philosophie", in: M. Riedel (Hg.), *Rehabilitierung der praktischen Philosophie*. Bd.1, Freiburg: Rombach Verlag, 1972, S. 343.

damer jedoch kritisiert, dass er die Zeitlosigkeit und Universalität des Wertes ignoriert und den Weg zum Relativismus und Nihilismus öffnet (obwohl er selbst gegen den Relativismus ist). In diesem Zusammenhang wurde häufig auf Jürgen Habermas' Kritik an Gadamer verwiesen. Tatsächlich wurde Gadamers Rezeption in China von mehreren berühmten Debatten um ihn herum begleitet, nicht nur mit Habermas, sondern auch mit Jacques Derrida in der deutsch-französischen Debatte und mit Emilio Betti in der ontologisch-methodologischen Debatte, um nur einige zu nennen. Man könnte sagen, dass die Beschäftigung mit Gadamer zugleich eine Verdeutlichung seines Platzes in der Entwicklung der zeitgenössischen kontinentalen Philosophie ist.

Der Einfluss Gadamers auf die chinesische Wissenschaft spiegelt sich außerdem in seiner exemplarischen Bedeutung für den Aufbau einer chinesischen Hermeneutik wider. Als spezifische Richtungen der chinesischen Hermeneutik können wir die „schöpferische Hermeneutik" von Wei-Hsun Fu, die „Onto-Hermeneutik" von Chung-Ying Cheng, die „Hermeneutik der Lehre der Menschlichkeit" von You-Zheng Li und die „Hermeneutik der Tugend" von De-Rong Pan nennen. Was aber im vorliegenden Beitrag erläutert wird, ist einer der grundsätzlichen Wege der chinesischen Hermeneutik, nämlich die Hermeneutik der Klassiker. Diese Idee geht auf die letzten Jahre des 20. Jahrhunderts zurück, in denen Chun-Chieh Huang und Yi-Jie Tang sie in verschiedenen Kontexten hervorbrachten und damit in der akademischen Gemeinschaft große Aufmerksamkeit erregten. Es gibt zwei Hauptmotivationen für den Aufbau einer chinesischen Hermeneutik der Klassiker: die eine basiert auf der kritischen Reflexion über die westliche Hermeneutik, einschließlich der philosophischen Hermeneutik Gadamers, und dem Versuch, sich auf das traditionelle chinesische Denken zu berufen, um deren Unzulänglichkeiten zu überwinden; die andere basiert auf der Forderung nach der Modernisierung der chinesischen Tradition der Interpretationen, um die Hermeneutik der Klassiker zu etablieren und sie zu einem wichtigen Teil der zeitgenössischen Hermeneutik zu machen. Auf dem letztgenannten Weg können zwei Modelle unterschieden werden. Das erste Modell konzentriert sich auf die Methodologie der Hermeneutik der Klassiker und versucht, die chinesische Tradition von klassischen Interpretationen zu systematisieren und zu theoretisieren; das zweite Modell basiert auf der philosophischen Hermeneutik Gadamers und es schlägt vor, dass die chinesische Hermeneutik der Klassiker auf einer ontologischen Ebene konstruiert werden sollte, vertreten insbesondere durch Nai-Qiao Yang und Hai-Feng Jing.

Mit dem Fortschreiten der Forschung erkennt die wissenschaftliche Gemeinschaft jedoch allmählich, dass der Ansatz bei der Trennung von Methodologie und Ontologie ein „Vorurteil" ist, das auf die zeitgenössische Entwicklung der chinesischen Hermeneutik nicht vollständig anwendbar ist. Qing-Liang Li schlägt stattdessen das *Dao des Auslegens* vor, das versucht, auf der Grundlage der Dualität des Dao eine grundlegende Brücke zwischen Methode und Ontologie zu schlagen und so eine umfassende Theorie der chinesischen Hermeneutik der Klassiker zu entwickeln. Die Hermeneutik beginnt mit der Methode und endet mit der Philosophie: Ohne die Vision der Philosophie bleibt die Hermeneutik eine Disziplin und eine Kunst; ohne die methodologische Grundlage kann die Hermeneutik zu einer Art metaphysischer Besinnung werden, die nicht in der Lage ist, ihre praktische Bedeutung für die humanistische Kultur zu verwirklichen.

Es zeigt sich, dass der Aufbau einer chinesischen Hermeneutik der Klassiker von einem Erwachen des Selbstbewusstseins und der Autonomie der chinesischen Wissenschaftler begleitet wird. Als Handing Hong im Jahr 2001 den hundertjährigen Philosophen Gadamer besuchte, wies dieser auf die Einzigartigkeit des Chinesischen als Sprache und auf dessen Bedeutung für die zukünftige Weltgemeinschaft hin. Dies ist zweifelsohne ein wichtiger Anhaltspunkt für die Entwicklung der chinesischen Hermeneutik. Beim Aufbau der chinesischen Hermeneutik der Klassiker sollen einerseits die chinesische Erfahrung und die chinesischen Besonderheiten der Hermeneutik hervorgehoben werden, andererseits sollte man jedoch auch auf eine universelle Hermeneutik abzielen, d.h. am Aufbau eines globalen hermeneutischen Diskurses mitwirken und die chinesische Weisheit in die Zukunft der menschlichen Gemeinschaft einbringen.

Hongjian Wang